D1075266

GOLF magazine's WINNING POINTERS
from the PROS

GOLF magazine's

Instruction Editors: GENE SARAZEN,

Illustrations by: LEALAND GUSTAVSON,

WINNING POINTERS
from the PROS

PEGGY KIRK BELL

DOM LUPO and others

HARPER & ROW, PUBLISHERS, NEW YORK

WINNING POINTERS FROM THE PROS. *Copyright © 1959, 1960, 1961, 1962, 1963, 1964, 1965 by Universal Publishing & Distributing Corp. Printed in the United States of America. All rights reserved. No part of this book may be used or reproduced in any manner whatsoever without written permission except in the case of brief quotations embodied in critical articles and reviews. For information address Harper & Row, Publishers, Incorporated, 49 East 33rd Street, New York, N. Y. 10016.*

LIBRRY OF CONGRESS CATALOG CARD NUMBER: 65-15412

CONTENTS

INTRODUCTION

In 1960, when the first *Golf Magazine* book, *Pro Pointers and Stroke Savers* was published, Charles Price, then editor of *Golf,* said in the introduction, "Sixty-one of these pros—almost all of them championship caliber—have passed on a lifetime of observation and study to form this book, one that I think will prove unique in the considerable library of golf." And unique it was. In the years that followed, many of the tips contained in *Pro Pointers* have become a standard part of most good golfers'—pro and weekend amateurs alike—shot repertory.

Now five years later, a second collection of score-improving tips from the world's finest pros, covering the entire game is here. As with the first volume, the suggestions and tricks-of-the-trade contained in this book have evolved on the same ruthless testing ground—the American pro tour.

But there is a difference. In five years, the tour has gotten immeasurably tougher what with bigger purses, more tournaments and, inevitably, more competitors. Unquestionably the pro today has to keep up with the new developments and indeed, develop his own new ways of making shots if he expects to make even an occasional appearance in the winner's circle.

As has always been true, the weekend golfer eventually becomes aware of these new developments and techniques, and incorporates them into his game. The *Golf Magazine* books, we feel, have contributed to the speed of this awareness and to the improvement of the weekend golfer's game.

To make up this volume, over sixty-odd of the best shot-makers contributed pointers which have worked particularly well for them—both in and out of competition. In a few years, no doubt, these techniques too, will become a standard part of the wise golfer's game.

July 1965 The Editors

GOLF magazine's WINNING POINTERS
from the PROS

I. REVIEWING THE FUNDAMENTALS

If the fundamentals mean a great deal to the professionals, they should mean even more to the weekend golfer. If you understand why a certain grip or address produces a certain result you will be much better able to deal with your wandering shots. For here truly is the easiest way to play well with a minimum of practice. So why not spend some time here reviewing the fundamentals? They're not as exciting or as colorful as some of the sections that follow but don't forget an awareness of the essentials is the first step to those stroke-cutting shots.

1. THINK! BEFORE YOU PLAY

By Bob Goalby

Grooving the perfect golf swing does not necessarily guarantee a good game. For if the owner does not adequately combine his physical talent with a sound mental approach to every shot, he may still "look" like a hacker on the score card.

Since golf is not an easy game, it doesn't make sense to make it tougher by trying to execute shots beyond your capabilities or by ignoring the numerous hazards that generally confront you.

Selecting the proper club in the rough, teeing the ball lower against the wind and using the putter on certain occasions from the apron are just a few ways in which a golfer can improve his game. In short, he'll play better golf if he "plays it smart." Here then are some suggestions which I hope will help the thinking man.

PREPARING FOR THE ROUND Do your practice putting before you go to the practice tee. The reason is that if you do a half-hour of practice putting immediately before you tee off, your back muscles are likely to be stiff from stooping over.

For the weekend player, practice should be a limbering-up exercise. You should hit at least a couple of dozen balls just to loosen up, starting with the short irons and progressing to the driver. Since you're not under any pressure on the practice tee, you should make at least fair contact with the ball, and this should bolster your confidence for the upcoming round.

If your course doesn't have an area where you can hit full shots, then spend some time hitting short chip shots or at very least spend some time on the putting green. Remember some practice, no matter how little, is better than none at all.

Try to arrive at least 30 minutes before you are scheduled to tee off. Don't jump out of your car, rush over to the first tee and hit away. Allow sufficient time to get to the course. Your nerves won't be in tip-top shape if you have to battle heavy traffic and the clock in order to arrive in time.

3

ON TEEING UP   If I've seen a hole before, I already know where I want to play my tee shot. Any other player should, too. I make it a point always to tee my ball on the same side of the tee as the trouble. In other words, if there's a tight out-of-bounds to the right, I tee the ball on the right side so I'll be hitting away from the trouble.

On a wet course I tee the ball a little higher than I usually do to get more carry. Conversely, on a very dry course I tee the ball a little lower to get more roll.

If a fairway is very narrow, it pays to tee the ball a little lower and not to swing too hard. This encourages you to stay down on the ball better and to hit through it.

On tee shots I tee the ball a little forward of center so that I will catch it a little on the upswing. For best results, I'd advise playing the tee shot opposite the left heel.

The average player can save at least one stroke per round if he uses the correct club off the tee. He's convinced, in many instances, that he must use the driver. This is a misconception. If you are not hitting this club well, try the three-wood. This way you'll be much more certain of getting the ball into the air with more carry. There's only about a ten-yard difference between the two clubs anyway. In winning the 1961 Colonial Invitational, Doug Sanders hit the driver only eight times during the entire four rounds.

When hitting drives, use the club in which you have the most confidence. It's going to take at least two shots to get on the green anyway, so why not play safe and get on in two? Play the percentages. It pays.

By teeing the ball on the same side as the trouble, you provide yourself with a larger, safe hitting area.

HITTING FROM ROUGH   One error the average player often makes is trying to get too much distance from the rough, sometimes using a three- or four-wood where he should be using nothing stronger than a four-iron. When a wood strikes the rough, the heavy grass slows the clubhead. The average player can't muster enough clubhead speed, in many cases, to offset the effect of this heavy grass.

You would get better results if you were to use a mid-iron and employ more of an upright, chop-down swing that will get the ball airborne more quickly. Stay away from the two- and three-iron in the rough. You can hit a four-iron 175 yards out of the rough, and you'll stand a much better chance of getting the ball out.

WHEN IN TROUBLE   Reckless gambles add needless strokes. When you are in trouble, survey the situation. If there's a chance of making a high score if you gamble, then don't. One stroke lost isn't going to make much difference in the final analysis. So if you are in trouble, take your medicine, play a safety shot into the fairway and try to salvage a par from there. Many times, 85-shooters wind up with 95 because they gambled when the odds were stacked against them. So play it safe on those holes where it's easy to take an eight or nine. You'd be surprised how often players on the tour will do just this. After all, if you play a safety shot into the fairway and knock your third on, you can still hole a 20-footer for a par.

TRAP SHOTS   To play trap shots successfully, you must have the proper equipment, namely the sand iron. Many players make the mistake of trying to hit the ball too close to the pin from a trap. The objective if you are in a trap is simply to get the ball on the green. This applies to the average player, of course. Now on courses where it's possible to putt out of traps that don't have lips, it's advisable to do so.

Any qualified professional can explain the sand shot to you. With good instruction from him and a little practice, you should be able to play this shot reasonably well within an hour.

I like to work my feet down into the sand when addressing the ball in a trap. If I don't do this, I get the feeling I'm floating on eggs and am afraid to swing. I make a much better swing and have much more assurance when I plant my feet about an inch and a half deep in the sand.

I aim two inches behind the ball on almost all trap shots with the blade

6

When in the trap, work your feet into the sand for sure footing. Aim about two inches behind the ball and open the blade about 45 degrees.

open 45 degrees. I take a slow, lazy swing, picking the club up a little going back, and I always follow through. As long as you hit two inches behind the ball and keep the club moving, it will skid under the ball and loft it out softly.

This shot requires courage. You must be certain not to quit when you contact the sand. Use a firm grip but don't try to hit the ball too hard. The more easily you get the club through the sand, the better the shot will be. In playing from the sand, I open my stance and employ very little body turn.

READING GREENS As a rule, bent grass greens don't have much grain so if you play on bent greens, grain shouldn't be too much of a problem. On the other hand, Bermuda greens, usually found in the South, have considerable grain.

Read the green from all angles. Knowing which way the ball will break is as important as the stroke itself.

Here's the best way to "read" them. If the green between your ball and the hole is shiny, the grain is *with* you, and the green will putt about 33 percent faster than normal. If the green is dull, the grain is *against* you and the green will be about 33 percent slower than usual.

If you putt Bermuda greens, you must be able to read them to be successful. On many seaside courses the grain goes toward the water. On mountain courses the grain often goes toward the mountains.

CHIPPING   Any time you're within six feet of the green, the straighter the face of the club you chip with, the better off you'll be. Don't use a pitching wedge from within ten feet of the green.

Under normal conditions, when I'm 30 feet from the hole and about six feet from the green, I use a six-iron, lofting the ball about one-third the distance and letting it roll the rest of the way. If the green runs downhill, I'll go to a seven-iron. If the shot is uphill, I'll use a five-iron so the ball will run a little more.

8

Chipping with low irons (three, four, etc.) allows you to roll the ball toward the hole in much the same way as you would if you were putting it.

One of the key factors in successful chipping is a firm left hand. Keep the last three fingers of the left hand very firm as you hit down and through the shot. This will prevent a scooping action and provide better roll.

At address on a chip shot, I play the ball a little behind center, keeping my hands ahead of the ball and most of my weight on the left side, especially on the left heel.

In chipping, always grip right down close to the shaft of the club. Many players take too big a swing, then slow down when they get to the ball. When you choke down on the club, you can take a short swing, hit the ball firmly and accelerate through the ball. The choked grip also affords better control of the club.

ADJUSTING TO TROUBLE   It's important to know where trouble is and to play accordingly. For example, if there's an out-of-bounds, a canyon, creek or woods over a green, don't overclub. That is, always take the club that, if hit perfectly, will put you on the green. Never take more club and say: "I'm only half-hitting the ball today, so I'd better make sure I get up there." If you do this when there's trouble over the green, you'll probably catch the ball on the button, go into trouble and take an eight or nine.

On the other hand, if there's a gaping trap in front of the green and no trouble behind the green, the opposite line of reasoning applies. Then you should take plenty of club, perhaps one more than you'd normally need to cover this distance. Then if you mis-hit the shot slightly, you can still catch the green or be hole-high. And if you should hit the shot perfectly, you'll go over the green but you won't be in as much, if any, trouble.

If you're in a bad lie, be extremely leery of a three- or four-wood. You'd be better off using a four- or five-iron and making sure you get the ball airborne. All too often, you'll top or skull wood shots from bad lies. The two-iron is also a hard club for the average player to hit from good lies, let alone bad situations.

THE FIVE-WOOD   Long irons are so hard for the average player to hit well, because of lack of loft on the face and the fact that they are not hit very often, that I think he'd be well advised to carry a five-wood. This club will get the ball in the air faster and bring it down more softly than a two-iron. And the five-wood is a much easier club to hit because the face is more lofted.

10

When I won the 1960 Coral Gables and 1961 Los Angeles Opens, I used a five-wood. I have replaced the four-wood in my set with this club and now feel that everyone should have a five-wood. The average player should leave his two-iron home.

PLAYING IN THE WIND Even the best players usually have their troubles in the wind. However, there are ways to minimize the effect the wind will have on your scores. For example, when driving into the wind, tee the ball low so you'll keep it below the tree line and won't encounter as much wind. With the wind, tee the ball higher than usual to take advantage of the following wind.

If there's a cross wind, don't try to fight it. If the wind is blowing left to right, aim a little to the left of the target and let the wind bring the ball in.

There's a tendency to grip the club more tightly when playing against the wind. This is a mistake. It is more advisable to loosen the grip just a little. Most players tend to swing too hard against the wind. Loosening the grip a little will curb this tendency. You don't swing as hard when you loosen your grip.

When hitting against the wind, choke down about an inch on the grip,

Teeing the ball high will help you gain more distance when the wind is at your back and when the fairways are wet and thick.

Tee the ball lower when hitting into the wind.

11

take more club and make sure you make solid contact. A solidly hit shot is far less affected by wind than a mis-hit shot.

Good players keep the ball low in the wind. Choking up on the club will help you do this.

PLAYING IN COLD WEATHER The key here is to keep the hands warm. This can be done with hand-warmers, by wearing gloves between shots or simply by keeping the hands in the pockets. As for apparel, avoid binding clothing and bulkiness. I like to wear a sweater or two, a windbreaker and wool trousers.

I feel a rubber grip is best in the cold because leather sometimes gets slick. The leather grip is good in hot weather, though. The all-weather rubber grip is best for all seasons, in my opinion.

In hot weather be sure to keep the hands dry. If you wear a glove, change it when it gets wet and let it dry.

ADJUSTING TO SEASONS In the summer the sun-baked ground is hard. So tee the ball a little lower to take advantage of the extra roll.

In the fall the average player does not get enough carry. When it is cold or wet, he is better off if he uses a slightly more lofted club. For example, instead of hitting a three-wood off the fairway, try a four-wood because with it you'll have a better chance of getting the ball higher into the air and it'll travel just as far as the three-wood shot.

VISUALIZING THE SHOT This, to me, is the same as planning the shot and is especially applicable on shots to the green. A player must have enough imagination to visualize what the shot is going to look like. For example, if he's hitting with the wind and there's no trouble in front of the green, he should be able to visualize the ball landing about ten yards short, taking a few bounces and rolling to the pin. Visualizing especially comes into play on the short shots.

A HELPFUL EXERCISE The forearms and wrists play a vital role in hitting a golf ball. To develop wrist and hand strength, try squeezing a small rubber ball. Most golfers are right-handed and have underdeveloped left sides. A player should try to develop his left side as much as possible. It would help if you'd use the left hand more often.

12

SOME ADDITIONAL HINTS   1. Don't use the one- or two-wood off the fairway unless the lie is exceptionally good.

Putting off the apron is often referred to as using the "Texas wedge." Using this shot correctly can save you strokes.

2. Don't be afraid to use the putter from just off the green when the fringe is short. Professionals use this shot a lot, especially in tight or sandy lies.

3. Always respect out-of-bounds, giving it as much room as possible.

4. In practice, spend more time hitting choked-down wedges, pitch shots and putts. The scoring area in golf is within 100 yards of the green. The more time you spend on the shorter shots, the more your scoring will improve.

5. Don't tee up in the fairway just because "winter rules" permit you to. Always play the ball where it lies unless the lie is very bad. Even then, avoid extremes in teeing it up. Taking preferred lies does a player's game

13

more harm than good because this practice encourages a scooping action that is bad for one's game.

6. On par-threes, always use a tee because the ball will come off it the same way every time. If you set it on grass, you're getting into a more unpredictable situation because the ball will react differently when hit from sandy soil than from firm soil, for example. Use of the tee always provides more consistency.

7. Take one more club when hitting to elevated greens and one less club when hitting from an elevated position to the green.

8. Make sure you take enough club. Many players don't because they overrate their strength. The average player will help himself if he takes one more club on shots where he is unsure of himself. By not swinging as hard, he'll make more solid contact.

9. Don't take too big a bite on doglegs. It doesn't pay except in extraordinary cases. Play the hole as it was designed, and you'll have a much better angle to the green for your second shot.

10. If you're fading, play the fade by allowing for it. Don't change your grip and swing during a round. Wait until you get to the practice tee or to your professional before making changes.

11. You can play a ball out of water as long as the water does not cover the ball. If it is submerged, forget about trying to play it.

12. Every player needs a little temper to keep him fired up, but too many of us let our tempers get the better of us. We get so mad we have trouble visualizing shots, and we just swing harder and harder. Try to keep your temper under control. This involves mental discipline.

13. Many players swing too hard and take too big a cut. Invariably, they lose control of the club at the top of the swing and sometimes even lose sight of the ball. To offset this tendency, choke up slightly on the club, don't swing quite as hard and shorten the backswing.

14. If you're having putting trouble, try choking down on the putter, spreading the feet more and using a "tap" stroke. You should get more "feel" this way.

15. Many touring professionals practice putting at night in their motel rooms. This exercise is very helpful as a means toward keeping the blade square, getting solid contact and developing "muscle memory" through repetition.

2. PRO POINTERS ON THE GRIP

IT STARTS WITH THE GRIP

By Tommy Bolt

I have to rate a faulty grip as the most common cause of bad golf. *To get a good hit, you need to develop clubhead speed, and to get clubhead speed, you must use your hands.* Too many high-handicappers place their hands on the club in a weak position, that is, with both hands turned too much to the left with the thumbs on top of the shaft. The golfer will then pick up the club on his backswing and, in so doing, has little chance of hitting the ball well. Besides, this grip encourages a slice—a curve most golfers could do without! *Place the left hand on the club so that you see about two and a half knuckles, with the thumb on the top right-hand side of the shaft. Then grip with the right hand, with its thumb on the top left-hand side of the shaft. The "V's" formed between the forefingers and thumbs of both hands should point upward to the same spot, somewhat right of the chin.* You can even move both hands still further to the right —say, with the "V's" pointing to the right shoulder—until you start hitting solidly, as this position almost forces you to take the club back inside. If you start to hook too much, you can gradually move the hands back toward the top of the shaft. *But remember: to play good golf, you must use your hands, and using your hands effectively starts with a good grip.*

16

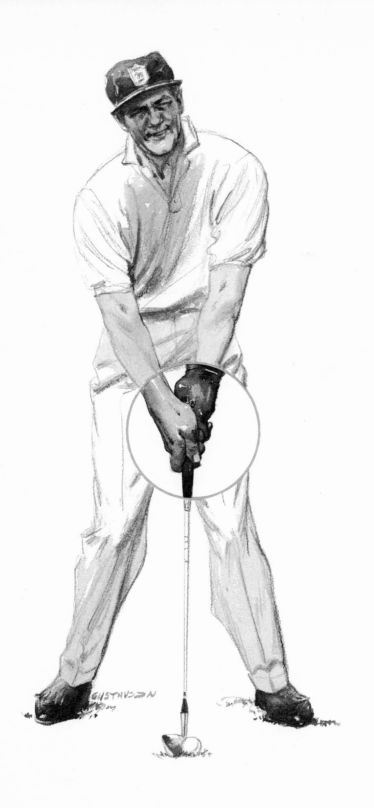

KEEP YOUR GRIP FIRM

By Tommy Strafaci

To groove a swing that will get more distance, exert the same amount of pressure with your hands throughout the swing. It is essential that you take enough time to do this at the beginning, when you first take hold of the club. A majority of all the hitters I have noticed, big or small, seem to grab the club without a careful check to see whether they are holding it correctly, and then they whip into the backswing too quickly. Maybe it is because my course (Dyker Beach) is the busiest in the world, and everyone is in such a hurry to get out to play that they overlook this fundamental. But I suspect it happens everywhere. This habit might be acquired by golfers who come into the game after having played baseball, where it is natural to open the hands and then regrip for power as part of the routine. Avoid this mistake with the golf club, because *any loosening of the grip requires you to regrip, usually in the middle of your swing. The clubhead will loop and distance and control are lost.* To me, the only time golf shots are missed, whether by pro, amateur or beginner, is when this happens. *Guide the stroke through steady pressure on the club from start to finish and you'll swing with confidence.*

18

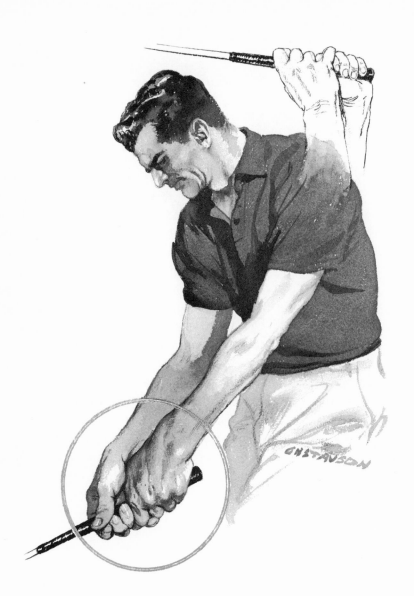

THE THUMB AND THE PALM

By Ian Crowe

The general attitude of higher-handicap players is that the grip is incidental to the swing. But, in truth, far from being incidental, the grip is an *integral* part of the swing. *Once the hands are together on the club, preparatory to making the swing, they should stay together until the completion of the swing.* "Gripping with the last three fingers" of the left hand is a popular explanation of the grip and is correct as far as it goes, but it is in itself insufficient. The left-hand grip consists of the last three fingers *plus half the palm*. As for the right, the expression "pinching with the thumb and forefinger," or emphasizing the function of the two middle fingers, clearly indicates this hand requires a finger grip, and this is true. But greatly overlooked, and to a great extent not even considered, is the part played by the thumb of the left in relation to the palm of the right. *The thumb should nestle in the palm of the right hand throughout the swing. By doing this, the hands will remain together. This is particularly important at the top of the swing where a loose grip can lead to a hit from the top.* By all means grip with the last three fingers and the palm of the left hand, and have a secure grip with the fingers of the right hand. But *the link between the two hands is provided by the thumb of the left hand staying in the palm of the right hand. At impact your hit will be more solid.*

20

CORRECTING HOOKS AND SLICES

By Bert Weaver

Practically every golfer, regardless of his proficiency, is afflicted with an occasional attack of hooking or slicing. It's especially frustrating when a golfer, after working hard to correct the trouble and thinking he has it licked, suddenly finds he just can't make the ball behave. It used to happen to me until I learned what to do about it. I have found that hooking usually occurs as a result of relaxing the left hand and that slicing often happens as a result of relaxing the right hand. I follow a simple and effective system to counteract these tendencies to hook and slice. *Whenever I start to hook, I concentrate on tightening the left hand as I address the ball. In the case of the slice, I tighten the right hand at address.* No golfer is beyond a hooking or slicing seizure. But it's encouraging to remember that when the hooking or slicing bug bites, there is an antidote.

THE GRIP

By Bob Goalby

One of the keys to a sound grip is to keep both hands as close together as possible. The club is held in the fingers and palm of the left hand and mainly in the fingers of the right. Be careful not to grip the club too tightly. A death grip causes the left wrist to lock and encourages picking the club up too abruptly on the backswing. *Two important don'ts: Don't loosen the grip at impact—and don't change the pressure of the grip during the swing.* I have seen some golfers who loosened their grip at the top of the swing and then regripped it at the start of the downswing. This can only lead to a pull or slice. Much has been written and said about the position of the "V's" formed by the thumbs and forefingers in the grip. I feel the two "V's" should point to the chin. This kind of grip seems to be suitable to the majority of golfers although hand sizes should be considered also. With small hands, the "V's" are in a better position when they point toward the right collarbone. *I prefer the overlapping grip to the interlocking mostly because I find the latter promotes tension. Keeping the hands close together allows them to work as a single unit and gives the left hand a better chance to control the usually stronger right.* The left hand should control the swing and the right should provide much of the power.

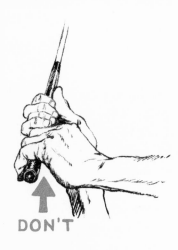

DON'T

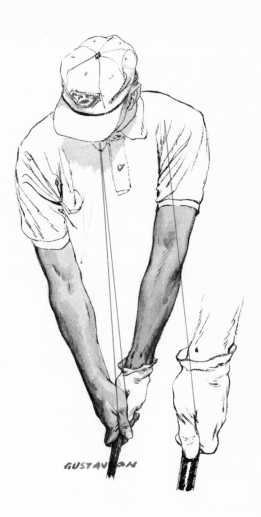

GUSTAVSON

3. PRO POINTERS ON ADDRESSING AND TEEING THE BALL

ADDRESSING THE BALL

By Dutch Harrison

Most golfers address the ball incorrectly, gripping the club with the left hand, setting the blade behind the ball and then placing the left foot. In placing the blade behind the ball with the left hand, the left shoulder is nearly always pulled lower than it should be. When the left shoulder is lower than the right, the player takes the club back "under" and gets into a "locked" position a little more than halfway through the backswing. By "under" I mean rolling the wrists counterclockwise on the backswing. By "locked" I mean in a position that makes it difficult to take the club back farther. *The right way to address the ball is to grip the club with the* RIGHT *hand and set the blade behind the ball, placing the* RIGHT *foot as you do. Then put the left hand on the grip and the left foot in place.* You'll find when you do this that the right shoulder will be lower than the left at address. Halfway through a practice backswing, take your right hand off the club. If you look as though you were going to shake hands with someone, you're in good position.

ALIGN YOURSELF TO A TARGET

By Bill Meyers

You have not completed your tee shot preparations until you have determined where you want your ball to stop and have checked on your alignment. This ritual should become a routine prerequisite to any shot, because only then will you begin to discipline yourself and your game. *In selecting a target, be fair with yourself. Visualize an area at least the size of a green that is within your capabilities to reach.* Remember that you can get just so much distance out of your clubs and no more. *Once the target is chosen, align yourself properly.* I recommend you sight the line of flight by walking up to the ball from the rear, then position your feet so that an imaginary line drawn between your toes (or heels) is parallel to your intended direction. *Guard against unknowingly aiming too much to the right, in what you may think is a desired closed stance.* A man might never become a top-rate golfer until he learns to swing the club from inside out, but this is not the way it is done, *because you risk blocking the left side, forcing you to pull your body and hands across the ball improperly.* Before teeing off, pick out a target area, check your alignment, square your stance and, when you stay with the shot, the correct action follows.

LINING UP THE SHOT

By Al Balding

Nothing can be more exasperating than to execute a shot perfectly only to watch it sail off line into trouble. This failure to properly line up the shot happens when inexperienced players take their stance as soon as they step up to the ball—before placing their club behind the ball. Thus the ball is often incorrectly positioned in relation to the stance. The flaw could be avoided if they were to alter their procedure in this fashion: (1) Walk to the shot. (2) Sole the clubhead behind the ball, aiming the bottom line of the clubface directly at the target. (3) *In the mind's eye, draw a line perpendicular to the line of flight from the clubhead to the correct spot between the feet for the particular club being used.* (4) Place first the left foot, then the right foot into the correct positions for the particular club, keeping the clubface directed at the target. (5) Execute the shot. Let these five steps become second nature to you and you'll hit fewer shots off line.

TEEING FOR DISTANCE

By Bob Goetz

The worst way to hit a drive if distance is your objective is to hit it "thin," or low on the clubface. *I solved this problem by teeing the ball much higher than most pros. I use a tee about two inches in length.* I'm not alone in this. Ed Furgol's tees are at least an inch and a half long. The way I look at it, teeing the ball low increases your margin for error. When the ball's teed low, it's more imperative that it be struck perfectly for best results. But if the ball's teed from one to two inches off the ground, you have a much greater tendency to play it farther forward and are therefore much more likely to catch it on the upswing. Hitting the ball on the up-stroke provides more distance for two reasons. First, by striking the ball on the upswing you get more overspin and therefore more roll on dry courses. Second, you get a higher trajectory and therefore more carry, which helps on wet courses.

TEE THE BALL HIGH

By Max Faulkner

I have observed both in America and England that the average player tees the ball too low, picks the driver up too abruptly on the backswing and chops down on the ball in order to get it airborne. In England I have used a very helpful practice exercise to combat this tendency. *Our tees have a hole in them, so it is possible to insert one into another. This I do so that the teed-up ball will sit three to four inches above the ground.* I instruct my pupils to take the driver around close to the ground and to sweep the ball off the tee. It takes a half-dozen hits or so on the practice tee to get accustomed to this, but you'll find the reward for the extra time and effort ample. I'll guarantee anyone who gives this exercise a good try 20 yards more carry on tee shots. The important thing is to tee the ball high, go back low and hit up and out. If you sweep under the ball, you'll know you have *not* performed the exercise correctly. The ball will merely drop to the ground. The prime requisites for success in this effort are a three-inch tee, willingness to work a little and patience.

TEE LOW TO AVOID HOOKING

By Gene Coghill

When severe trouble looms on the left of the fairway and a drive that hooks would be disastrous, I find it very helpful to tee the ball exceptionally low. *In addressing a ball that is low to the ground, I get a concept of a swing which does not permit the clubface to be closed or even completely square at impact. The rolling motion of the clubface tends to be minimized and the potential hook is changed to a straight ball or even a slice, since a slightly open face is necessary in order to assure getting the ball up properly.* In fact, even if the clubface is closed at impact, the low-teed ball has a better chance of staying in play as the hook spin will be lessened. Looking back, I don't recall ever having driven out of bounds to the left when I teed the ball low. *Conversely, if a hook is needed, you'll find it beneficial to tee the ball high enough so the clubhead will pass through without touching the ground, and the rolling of the clubface won't be impeded and a right-to-left spin can be imparted to the ball.*

TEE IT UP CAREFULLY

By Ed Furgol

Would you believe it if I told you that your slice was caused by the way you tee up the ball? It could be true. *Teeing the ball is like putting styles: It's individualistic and varies as each person's perspective varies.* Golfers who have the feeling of hitting under and through or on a high trajectory like to see the ball well off the ground. *The high tee, then, is recommended for those who stay behind the shot well or remain a little longer on the right side.* They *sweep* through, as compared to those who prefer to look at a ball just off the ground because they *hit* through. *If you can move to your left side smoothly, or if you tend to hit down on the ball (and get away with it), then tee it low.* Where does the slice come in? Low-ball hitters generally fade the ball, because they will open the face of the club at impact to conform to the terrain, as customarily happens when a driver is used from the fairway. Conversely, a ball that is teed high will encourage a hook. For those who feel that it helps to tilt the tee slightly when playing downwind, do so. Any idiosyncrasy is healthy as long as it is believed. *But definitely use a tee on the par-threes. Your "lie" will always be good, the height can be adjusted to personal taste and uniform contact can be made every time.*

USE A BRASSIE FROM THE TEE

By Eli Marovich

When your driving goes sour, should you change your grip, your swing, your stance? No, change your club. That is, switch to the brassie, the No. 2 wood. Modern-day golf equipment is better balanced than ever before, but the accent on big clubs sometimes gives the player the wrong idea. He gets to think that the bigger the head on the club, the easier it is to hit the ball. In my opinion, the reverse is true, and *when I'm asked if it would be all right to use the brassie instead of a driver when the shots begin to stray, I always give my full endorsement. Drivers usually have a square shape with little loft (about 10 to 11, occasionally 12 degrees). This often creates a mental block to the golfer,* who feels he has to make near-perfect contact with the ball for a good hit, and he works too hard trying to force his swing and get the ball airborne. *The brassie, however, is an easier club to handle, offers more margin for error and more accuracy with almost as much distance. Its loft is plainly visible and the player has the feeling that the ball will go up when hit without any "help" from his body. The result is that he swings through in a manner that would be ideal if the driver were used.* Now, I'm not saying to throw the No. 1 wood away. But don't use it until you can hit consistently with the No. 2 wood.

KEEP YOUR TEE SHOTS IN PLAY

By Billy Casper

Use the teeing area to give yourself as much of the fairway to land in as possible. *This would mean that if you are a left-to-right player—and more golfers do slice than hook, it seems—always hit your tee shot from the extreme right side of the tee. Move all the way to the right and take your stance so that you are aiming for the left side of the fairway. If you tend to hook, the spot for you to tee the ball would be on the extreme left-hand side and then square off your stance so that your direction of flight favors the right side of the fairway.* This seemingly simple maneuver of placing the tee in the proper spot can help cut strokes off your score before you even lay wood to the ball. By utilizing the launching pad in this manner, only the wildest slice or hook will fall out of play, and nothing adds to golfing pleasure more, unless it's a series of one-putt greens, than staying out of trouble. Now, if by happy chance you neither slice nor hook but always hit the ball down the middle of the fairway, it doesn't make any difference where you tee the ball. But if you are that straight, I suggest you turn pro and tee it up with us on the tour.

GOLF EXTRA:
WATCH YOUR FEET

By C. W. Griffin, Jr.

Sometime, while waiting on the first tee, focus your gaze on the footwork of the golfers teeing off. In the varied skips and hops you will see the basic steps of jigs, sailor's hornpipes and folk dances, and maybe even the mash potato and even less edible foot-scrapings that have replaced dancing for today's teenagers. One of the most common golfing steps is the tango sidestep, a version of the late Al Simmons' foot-in-the-bucket baseball swing. Executing this step, a right-handed golfer initiates his collapsing downswing with a quick, jerky step to the left, and slumping in straddle-legged disgust, morosely glares at his topped ball bounding drunkenly down the fairway.

The generally sad results of these golfing jitterbugs should convince any reasonable observer that smooth, balanced footwork is quite literally the foundation of a good golf swing. Moreover, you can correct faulty footwork more directly by conscious mental effort than some other actions of the swing that are governed more by reflex.

As an indispensable first step, invest in a pair of spiked shoes. To balance yourself against the thrusting weight shifts of a full swing, you need spikes, or at least deep-ribbed, rubber-soled shoes. A surprising number of public links players overlook this obvious point; I have seen many sliding around in ordinary leather-soled shoes.

UNDERMINING THE FOUNDATION Having hurdled this preliminary obstacle to good balance, turn your attention to the position at address. First, some advice on the width of stance. The proper distance between the feet entails a compromise between two conflicting needs. The closer the stance, the easier it is to achieve smooth footwork for the weight shift and pivot. On the other hand, the wider the stance, the easier it is to maintain balance. Most golfers fail to reconcile these considerations in changing their stance for different shots. Since maintaining balance for a drive

44

is more difficult than for a 50-yard pitch shot, the drive obviously requires a wider stance. Yet many golfers use nearly the same width of stance for every shot, when they should reduce the distance between the feet as the length and arc width of the swing diminish. Proper width of stance for different golfers can vary considerably, but here is a good general rule:

Keep the stance as narrow as possible consistent with good balance.

To demonstrate the validity of this rule, try swinging a club first with your feet as close together as possible, then with your feet as far apart as possible. In the first position you will have maximum freedom of motion for weight shift and pivot, with knees free for easy movement. In the second position your knees will lock under the sheer structural necessity of functioning as the legs of a roughly equilateral triangle supporting the body. Your pivot and weight shift will be severely restricted. Moreover, your whole body will drop closer to the ground, flattening and therefore constricting the arc of the swing. Despite the problem of balance, I think you will find that you can swing harder with the feet-together stance than you can with the straddle-legged stance.

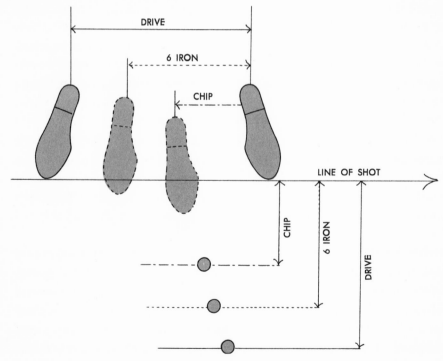

The address changes slightly for each club. Note the position of the ball in relation to the left foot, and that the right is drawing closer as the stance is opened.

45

Next is the problem of how far to stand from the ball. Here the common error again entails a failure to adapt the stance to the club length and the arc of the swing. Too many golfers stand too far from the ball on a drive, and as the club length shortens, the magnitude of this error increases. Some golfers stand almost as far from the ball for a pitch shot as they do for a drive. This tenses the arms and upsets the coordinated thrust of the right arm which should brush close by the right hip as the clubhead enters the hitting zone. As the club length decreases with increasing loft, and the arc of the swing becomes tighter and more upright for short irons and pitch shots, you must obviously stand closer to the ball.

Standing too far from the ball ordinarily places too much weight on the toes and tensions the backs of the legs, which must then balance the golfer like a bent model of the leaning tower of Pisa. The leaning-tower golfer will often find himself hitting the ball on the heel of the clubface and pitching forward during follow-through. This will usually cause a slice. Conversely, the golfer with his weight on both heels, will probably find himself hitting the ball on the toe and smother hooking and falling backward.

A finer point concerns the question of open, square or closed stance. An "open" stance has the right foot placed across the line of the shot; a "square" stance has both feet parallel to this line; and a "closed" stance has the left foot placed across the line. The stance should open from a slightly closed or square stance for a drive to an open stance for wedge shots. Moreover, since for short shots there is no need to turn the right toe outward to facilitate the pivot, the right foot should turn progressively inward as the stance width and shot length decrease. For chip shots it should be aligned parallel to the left foot. This parallel alignment of the right foot, with the right knee bent inward, restricts the tendency toward superfluous swaying, a common error of those who take too wide a stance for short shots.

Another common error is to assume a stance facing square toward the ball, with the hips aligned parallel to the direction of the shot and both knees locked or bent in the same position. To see why such a stance is wrong, think of the body position at impact. Flinging the club through the ball requires a rather full hip turn to the left, with the right elbow brushing by the right hip and the flexed leg pouring in power. To smooth the path of the swing toward the correct position at impact, your stance

46

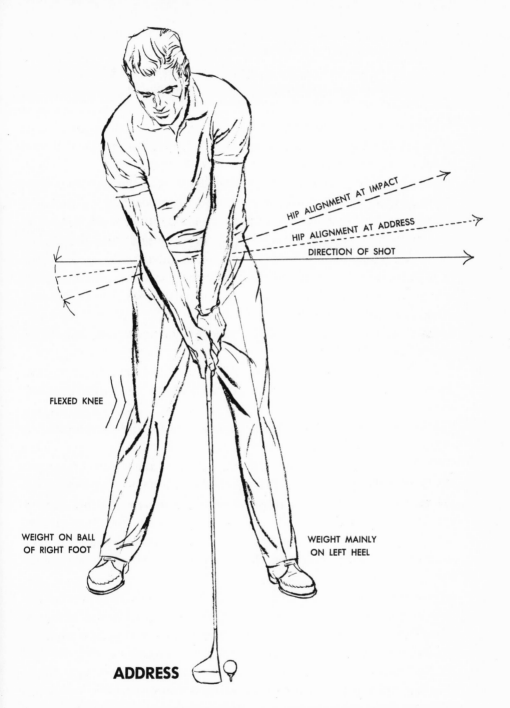

HIP ALIGNMENT AT IMPACT

HIP ALIGNMENT AT ADDRESS

DIRECTION OF SHOT

FLEXED KNEE

WEIGHT ON BALL
OF RIGHT FOOT

WEIGHT MAINLY
ON LEFT HEEL

ADDRESS

A good golf swing has a compact stability in which the major body movements are lateral (weight shift) and torsional (pivot).

at address must approach the position at impact. Aligning the hips parallel to the direction of the shot at address partly destroys the function of the backswing, which stores torsional energy later released as the body spring unwinds during the downswing.

BUILDING THE FOUNDATION   For the proper position at address, turn your hips slightly counterclockwise, i.e., turn your left hip slightly away from the ball, your right hip toward the ball. Though neither leg should be straight, this hip turn will naturally exaggerate the right knee bend toward the ball. Note, however, that the proper position at address is a compromise between orienting the swing for the full hip turn at impact and an easy start for the backswing. Thus your counterclockwise hip turn at address is much less than the full hip turn at impact.

Maintaining balance at this proper position at address requires a different distribution of weight. Bear in mind three things:

1. Distribute weight about equally on each leg.

2. Turn knees slightly inward so the weight bears somewhat on the inside edges of the feet.

3. To a considerable degree, distribute weight on the ball of the right foot; to a lesser degree, on the heel of the left foot. (Keeping the weight on the ball of the right foot keeps the right leg "alive," ready to pour power into the shot. Transferring the weight to the right *heel* during the backswing is *death*.)

The most difficult footwork action is the roll of the left foot. You must not lift the heel too far clear of the ground. A good golf swing has a compact stability in which the major body movements are lateral (weight shift) and torsional (pivot). Since it raises the whole body, allowing the left heel to rise an inch or two above the ground introduces into the swing a superfluous bobbing motion, destroying its smooth efficiency. It ruins one's chances of setting the left heel before starting the downswing, the key to efficient use of the swing's stored energy. By setting the left heel before starting the downswing you can delay release of the swing's stored energy until the moment of impact. Failure to do so inevitably initiates the energy-dissipating action known as "hitting from the top."

The proper roll of the left foot accompanies a proper weight shift at the start of the backswing. Because of the old exaggerated taboo against swaying, many golfers fail to make the subtle hip shift and weight transfer required *before* pivoting. The weight transfer is essential to develop the

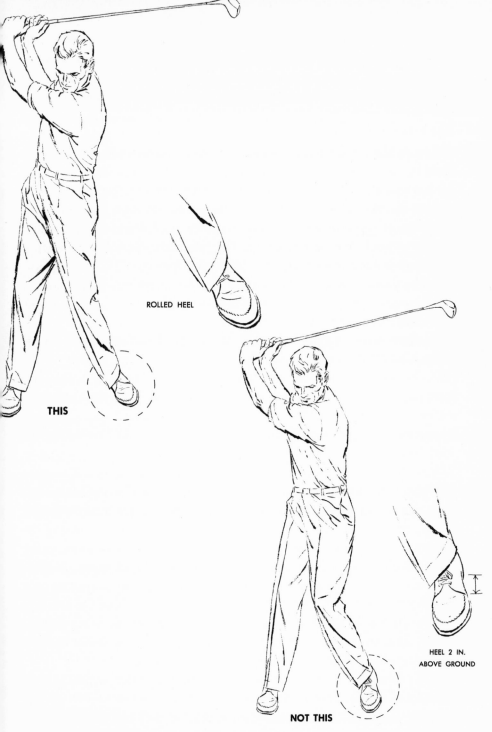

ROLLED HEEL

THIS

NOT THIS

HEEL 2 IN.
ABOVE GROUND

Roll the left foot on the backswing. Do not lift the heel too far off the ground.

swing's full potential power. At the start of the backswing, as the weight shifts to the right foot, the left knee should bend easily inward, and the left foot should merely roll about the inside edge of the ball of that foot. The heel should barely rise off the ground, even on a full swing. On short iron shots (say, eight-iron on up), the heel need not leave the ground at all.

This proper rolling action of the left foot is a compromise between two opposite extremes—the heel-raising rotating action about the toe, warned against earlier, and a lateral rolling about the inside edge of the *whole* foot. The latter action generally accompanies premature pivoting, in which the weight remains predominantly on the left foot and the left side buckles. This is commonly a fault of golfers who start the backswing from a tense, motionless position without a "forward press." The recoil from the forward press will generally accomplish the weight transfer to the right foot and facilitate the proper rolling action of the left foot about the *ball* of the foot.

Before starting the downswing, set the left heel and then let fly. With the start of the downswing, you have performed the last conscious act of the swing. If you find yourself falling forward or backward, with the symptoms mentioned earlier, look for sins committed elsewhere. To use a slightly mixed metaphor, if you start off on the wrong foot you can't change stride in the middle of the swing.

To develop the feel of good footwork assume a narrow stance (about eight inches clear between heels) and swing the club easily and continuously, alternating full backswings and downswings. Concentrate on keeping that left heel close to the ground so you can easily set it before starting the downswing.

Since so many vital actions depend on it, improving your footwork can automatically correct other flaws in your swing. As underpinning stabilizes a settling, cracking structure, good footwork smooths a creaking golf swing.

II.   EXECUTING THE SWING

Few of us are gifted with the natural swing of, say, Sam Snead. Conse-quently, the rest of us have to work harder to build a functional, repeating swing. (In short, a swing that works.) In the following section, some of America's most talented pros have contributed tips they've found reliable in grooving a repeating swing. We're sure they'll help you too.

4. BE SIMPLE, BE CONSISTENT

By George Buck

Golf can be as intricate or as simple a game as you want it to be, and because it can be approached from so many directions, it is always interesting if not always rewarding. But for everyone who has been able to reap golf's many benefits, there are hundreds of potentially fine players who don't have the patience to dig deep enough into the different theories —and they quit.

It is to this segment of the sports-minded, those who otherwise wouldn't give golf a chance to show its true value as an enjoyable pastime, that I direct this method of learning. I call it a short cut to consistency, because it will get you to hit better shots more quickly and more often. It has proved to be an inspiration and an education on how to hit the ball properly, for the beginner and the veteran alike. While it may not develop any Arnold Palmers overnight, it has guided many to championship caliber, and it will lead to lower scores, a step in the right direction, regardless of present handicap.

My tip to consistency is simple to describe and easy to understand, yet it continues to amaze not only those who have attended my clinics, but also the many who now play my way and report that they are "finally enjoying golf for the first time." The reasons for this overwhelming response, I believe, are that my method doesn't suggest a change in swing, or an immediate investment in a new set of clubs, or hours on the practice tee, or anything quite like that. It is designed only to eliminate those parts of the swing that have nothing to do with the actual hit, or in producing the hit, and it emphasizes just the areas that lead directly to what you —and everyone else—is looking for: accuracy and distance. With all unnecessary movements done away with and the mechanics of the swing reduced to the least number of parts, my pupils stand up to the ball with a mind uncluttered with useless, restrictive detail, and they are in a better frame of mind to play good golf.

Play ball off left foot, keep weight entirely on [l]eft side to eliminate any need to pivot. Three-quar[ter] backswing is controlled by anchored left h[eel.] There is no opening or closing of the clubface a[nd] no danger of any lateral sway.

At impact, body approximates address position, with arms and club shaft forming the letter "Y," which had moved away and returns to the ball in one unit. Head is steady, hands in perfect alignment, right elbow tucked in close.

The right side, made passive by concentration of the weight on left side, is easily released as clubhead whips into and through the ball with unusual force.

Concentration of weight on left side and short backswing set up clubhead acceleration, which reaches highest speed at impact, continues on through the ball and sends the hands up high. The result is consistent accuracy and distance.

Halfway through the swing, right knee is coming into the ball, but there'll be no awareness of any action from this side. Arms are fully extended, yet clubface has remained square. The pendulum-type swing is a combination of body and arms.

Better golf is not too much to expect from my method; nor is it too much to ask of yourself. *You can do it all by merely keeping your weight on the left side,* which is where it is when the ball is hit, *and by not pronating your wrists* and thus opening and closing the clubface.

There you have it. In essence, I advocate keeping your weight on the left side and keeping the clubface square *throughout your swing.* This applies to the tee shot, all fairway woods and irons including the wedge approach shot, and the putter. It means that once you have the "feel" for the swing, you can use it for every club in the bag, regardless of distance or difficulty.

I'm sure that it is no secret that the clubface must be square at impact if the ball is to be hit straight, and that the golfer must stay behind the ball if he is to hit into a strong left side and get more yardage. So why invite trouble *before you even hit the ball* by concerning yourself with how much weight to shift to the right side on the backswing, how far back to take the club, should the wrists bend inward or outward, is the angle of the clubface pointing to the sky, ground or halfway, are the knees flexed, is the weight on the inside or outside of the right foot, are the shoulders turned so that the back is facing the target, and did your heel come off the ground too much? Why make an important approach from either the fairway or trap or a treacherous putt any more difficult than it is by excess worrying and wondering?

Forget about such distractions and take a more thorough look into my method: Stand to the ball in a square-address position, with the ball opposite the left foot. Since your weight is almost entirely on the left side, you will be able to use the left leg as a swivel upon which you can make your turn, without any danger of a lateral sway on the backswing. Thus the left side acts as an axle, offering the same action as would pivoting from left to right and back again, but eliminating this movement entirely.

Grip the club as you would normally, with the hands exerting equal pressure but locked in position to act as a single unit. Tuck the elbows in close to the body as though held in place by an elastic band. Now the arms form the letter "V" and, together with the straight shaft of the club, they form the letter "Y." Turn this entire unit, which I'll continue to designate as "Y," to the right without cocking the wrists. There should not be any opening or closing of the clubface. The backswing will be restricted, and this is desirable, yet the arms will reach at least shoulder height, creating a large, sufficient arc. Keep the left heel on the ground, both eyes on the ball, and your takeaway will be limited to the three-

56

Grip club as you would normally, but be firm and gentle. (My grip is the inter-lock.) Elbows are tucked into body first, then arms are extended to give "feeling." The arms and the club together form the letter "Y," which should move from and to the ball in one unit. Keep wrists up to insure good posture and proper distribution of weight. When wrists are down, weight goes forward instead of being toward the heels where it belongs.

quarter backswing that this style calls for.

Coming back into the ball, the right side, which was made passive by concentrating the weight on the left, naturally fosters a good spring action and acts as a brace to this downward movement, and the clubface, still square to the line, hits against a left side that remains blocked. Clubhead speed is unbelievably fast as you whip into the ball with controlled force. All looseness, which only leads to inconsistency, is out. Firmness, for the big hit, is in. Together with rhythm, this is the formula for accuracy and distance.

Check again and note how my method keeps both the clubface square and the plane on a good, even line. First, to get the clubface flush to the ball, you have the ball positioned up forward, off the left foot, the left knee is flexed and the weight is on the left side, all providing the base or axle upon which the turn can be made without any swaying action. Second, to keep the plane smooth and efficient, you have the right arm tucked against the body; there is no pronation or wrist movement, the left heel is anchored and the grip, a two-handed one, is gentle but firm.

From beginning to end, this approximates a sweeping motion, or a part-body, part-arm swing. It can also be described as a pendulum move-ment, with the left shoulder being the hub or center point of the arc and the swing, from address, top of backswing, impact and follow-through, can be timed to a four-count as follows: One, Two, *Hit,* Four. In any event, the action is so controlled that you'll keep the ball in play more consistently and get more yardage more often than before, and you'll soon rave about the big difference in your game.

If, at first, this stance, arm, wrist and elbow position and restricted backswing feel awkward, don't get discouraged. Swing this way just ten times, and you will begin to work rhythm, timing and balance into the action, the movement will pick up speed, producing accuracy you can rely on, all the distance you will ever need, and more golf enjoyment than you ever thought possible.

A firm grip and the absence of any wrist pronation mean that the clubface will return to the ball exactly as it was at address. While all other shots which require accuracy call for a square face, the sand wedge, if it is to be open at impact, should be held in an open position at the start.

My instructional method completely coincides with my theory of successful putting:
Weight on left, clubface square, no wrist-break and pendulum-type swing.

5. PRO POINTERS ON THE BACKSWING

DON'T RUSH THE BACKSWING

By Johnny Pott

Whenever you get ready to "put the wood" to the ball, you certainly must be in the market for distance. And the most essential requirement for a successful wood shot is balance. Most golfers try to hit the ball too hard, which causes them to lose their balance and also lose distance and direction. If you remember that you hit the ball on the downswing and not on the backswing, you will take the club back slowly. *What's the use of jerking the club back fast when it has nothing to do with the hit?* All you take the club back for is to get ready to hit. The slower, the better. When you jerk the club too quickly from the ground, your hands move out of the slot, your rhythm and timing are impaired, and you're in trouble from the start. Make this movement slowly and smoothly. Complete the backswing right to the top—or when you no longer turn. As you finish the backswing, don't try to accelerate too fast. *Don't be in a hurry to come back to the ball. Just move into this vital area with both hands in control, the left hand leading, picking up speed as you go so that the clubhead will be moving fastest when contact is made. That's the only time—and in the only direction—that clubhead speed will do you any good.*

GROOVE THAT BACKSWING

By Billy Maxwell

The start of the backswing is what I call the "frame," and everything that subsequently occurs must be fitted into this frame until the follow-through is completed. The takeaway should be low and slow. *If you get your backswing started just right, so that it doesn't affect your balance or stance over the ball, you can control it more easily the rest of the way.* You should arrive at the end of your backswing in position to start the downswing with your hands together, and the whole action should be compact so that when you start down you are still in balance and still in good stance. Your chance of hitting the ball correctly is then extremely good. But the only way to achieve this satisfying sequence of events is to start exactly right. *There should, at the outset, be no excess motion or excess effort to impair the smoothness of the swing.* If you begin nice and easy when your stance is relaxed, your balance will remain good. Consequently, you should have no trouble keeping this balance as well as the correct motion throughout the swing.

CHECK YOUR BACKSWING

By John Young

The length of your backswing should not remain constant. To be effective, it has to differ from one day to the next. For example, it would change if a round of golf were played in the morning when you might be more refreshed than if you were to play after a tiring day of work, or when you are fighting a heavy wind, or when playing a tight course where accuracy is a premium. *The length of all backswings on tee shots should fall between the point where the left arm is parallel to the ground (minimum) and where the club shaft is parallel to the ground (maximum). A good checkpoint is to go back as far as you can to the maximum position without spraying the shot and without losing hand control of the club.* Your immediate goal is timing. The proper change in the length of the backswing can rid one of a slice, hook, push or scoop, and at the same time increase total distance. When I am giving a lesson, this is normally the first thing I check in my students, and quite often this one bit of concentration will turn a disgruntled golfer into a happy, confident one. Many professionals test their backswing on the practice tee before playing solely to develop their timing for that day's play. *I include myself among those who establish a different top (I call this my anchor point) to the backswing on any given day.* On weekends when I stand on the first tee and watch golfers of varying handicaps start their rounds, I am amazed how many are completely unaware of this mistake in their swing.

CUE THE BACKSWING

By Davis Love, Jr.

Most professionals agree that the first few feet of the golf swing are the most important. If you get started on the right track, then you'll very probably stay there throughout the entire swing. However, if the first motion is not correct, anything can happen. How do we get the right groove on the backswing? First, take the club back until the shaft parallels the ground. Now here's precisely where the checkpoint is reached. *Drop the club from the right hand and see if the right hand isn't in a perfect handshaking position.* If your club does not fall into this slot, you are probably troubled by a "flying" right elbow and a bad slice. Or else your elbow is jammed too tightly against the right side, restricting proper arm and shoulder movement. Try this checkpoint. You will find the cure for these faults surprisingly easy if you practice this little handshaking position exercise a few minutes before playing.

CONTROL THE RIGHT ELBOW

By Stan Wiel

The "flying elbow" is a common fault among high-handicap golfers, and in good measure it is the reason for their poor performance. The right elbow should stay close to the side all the way through the backswing, and *at the top of the swing the forearm and elbow should be pointing to the ground.* However, in search for power, the tendency is to let it sway way out, resulting in bad position at the top and a loss in efficiency and control coming into the ball. When the elbow comes away from the body, it forces a turn that produces an outside-in swing. That is, the clubface comes into the ball from outside the line, rather than from inside, where the power is. Keeping the right elbow close to the side may seem awkward at first, but it will pay off later in good length and control, especially on tee shots. *A good practice gimmick is to try to keep a handkerchief tucked under the right arm throughout the swing. You will probably feel a binding sensation, but it will help produce a good turn and get you on the track of the inside-out swing.* In so doing it also gets rid of that pesky slice which ruins many a game by the resultant loss in distance.

GROUNDING THE LEFT FOOT

By Frank Boynton

When a player with a sound grip and good mechanics misses a shot badly, the cause quite often is poor balance during the swing. One flaw I have to guard against as I play the PGA tour is "coming off the ball," or, in layman's language, moving my head laterally as I make my backswing. Such head movement makes it very difficult to make solid contact with the ball. Generally, the results will either cause a skied shot or a top. *To combat this tendency to "come off the ball," I keep my left foot flat on the ground throughout my swing. This enables me to turn my shoulders more fully and attain maximum power. At the same time, the planted left foot also helps keep the head in a steady position.* Before I resorted to this technique, I tried keeping my head perfectly still, but this restricted my swing and reduced my distance. I find it helpful now to address the ball with more of the weight on the left foot. On the backswing, I try not to think of my pivot but wind the body from the waist up until my shoulders have turned to the maximum. When I reach the top of my backswing, I have the feeling that the tip of my left shoulder is pointing toward the ball. *Keeping the left foot on the ground during the backswing will also make for greater tension between the shoulders and the hips, and this is what helps to build up power in the swing.* As simple as this idea is, it is easy to see that it can solve several problems that frequently occur.

6. PRO POINTERS ON THE DOWNSWING AND FOLLOW–THROUGH

STARTING THE DOWNSWING

By Dave Marr

An important part of the golf swing is keeping the arc of the club inside the intended line of flight during the backswing and first part of the downswing. *To do this, begin the downswing by shifting your hips and weight to your left side. In the first part of this maneuver, the hips will stay parallel to your line of flight for anywhere from four to eight inches depending on how supple you are. Moving the hips parallel and shifting the weight to the left side cause the right elbow to fall into the correct position, eliminating such bad habits as "hitting from the top," "casting," etc.* You will find this shifting of the weight will enable you to get your maximum power into the hitting area through the ball. If you move only slightly to the left side and your hip turns out of the way too quickly without the proper move parallel to the line of flight, you will "hit from the top" and cut across your intended line of flight. This produces a slice, with the weight remaining on the right foot as you finish. To learn the correct move you should begin with a short club such as a seven-iron. One way the average player can check this desired lateral movement is to note whether he finishes with the weight on his left foot and the divot pointing to his target.

LET THE HANDS PULL YOU

By Jean P. Stare

Do not spoil an otherwise sound swing by forcing the wrists to uncock early in the downswing in an attempt to throw the clubhead at the ball. This action is premature and gives the appearance of hacking or chopping at the ball. *You will eliminate the early-hit problem entirely if you get your hands pulling the clubhead through the ball and into the follow-through,* without strain. Remember, as you approach the bottom of the swing, you are only half through. You might have heard that the best way to eliminate casting (early breaking of the wrists) is to imagine you are trying to hit the ball with the butt of the club handle. While this advice is good, it doesn't go far enough. I have found that most golfers, when they think their hands have reached the "butt hand-to-ball" position and feel the clubhead dragging behind, will snap their wrists in a faulty effort to recoup. It is far better for the golfer *not* to think of snapping his wrists. *Continuous pulling of the hands will automatically allow centrifugal force to uncock them, swinging the clubhead down, into and through the ball. This pulling theory is evident everyday by the trick-shot artists who, with their hinged shafts, rubber hose shafts and chain shafts prove that centrifugal force must be the key to timing and clubhead speed.*

EXTENDING THE IMPACT ZONE

By Jacky Cupit

Hitting through the ball without pause or without lessening the impetus of the clubhead is absolutely necessary for low score and a sound game. To quit either before or after making contact with the ball will not only rob you of distance, but will also very likely give you a smothered hook or a big round slice. *Shifting your weight well forward to the left side and left foot is essential to getting through the ball.* George Bayer shifts his weight so completely target-wise that his left foot rolls over *after* impact. But at the precise moment of impact his weight, as is the case with most of us, is solidly on the right side, while the left foot is planted flat on the ground. I try to keep my weight slightly behind the shot, and as my hips move toward the target, my shoulders are moving away from it. The head must remain steady throughout the swing and, after impact, the clubhead must follow the intended line of flight as long as possible. Then the right wrist will naturally roll over the left reducing the strain; the hands should—and will—finish high.

DON'T MOVE OFF THE BALL

By Joe Redanty

The most violated motion in golf today is the one known as coming off the ball. Usually the result of being overly anxious to hit, it is an error that plagues both the professional and beginner alike. Simply, it is the mistake of hitting the ball on its equator and sending it screaming three to four yards off the ground, half hit. This error can occur with any club from the driver to the wedge and is often incorrectly diagnosed as looking up, taking the eyes off the ball or picking up the shoulders. *Really, it's the reverse, if anything. It's caused by starting the downswing with a stiff right leg which pushes the right shoulder up, moves the right elbow out away from the side, and forces the hands to release too early.* To overcome this fault, press forward toward the ball with the right knee as the club starts descending. This begins an automatic chain re-action: *as the right knee bends into the shot, the right heel releases from the ground to allow the weight shift to take place, the hands are prevented from uncocking too soon, the right elbow gets tucked in close to the right hip, the right shoulder stays under the left and squares the club-face as you enter the hitting area swinging from the inside.* Get into the correct slot by pressing forward with the right knee early in the downswing and you'll be off to a good start.

WRONG

GUSTAVSON

EASE UP WITH THE LONG IRONS

By Frank Strafaci

Long-iron play is regarded as the most difficult part of golf, *yet if you will just swing as usual and not consciously struggle for distance, you'll be surprised at how much more distance you will get.* The long irons seem difficult to play because they have little loft, and there is a natural feeling that the ball has to be "helped." So you hit too hard and get away from your normal swing. It is simply a matter of concentration. *Forget you are looking for distance and swing the club. You'll be surprised what the long iron will do for you.* Faced with a long-iron shot, most players tighten up. *They have hit the shot badly even before they start.* Too many times, the player is inclined to feel that with the straighter-faced clubs he has to *get it airborne. So he tries to help the ball up and, in so doing, forgets to swing, scoops at it and too often hits behind the ball.* An added hazard in hitting the long irons is that you usually are trying to reach the green, so you try to steer the ball around those yawning traps in the distance. *All this does is complicate matters for you by adding to your tension* and to the feeling that you have to guide the ball as well as hit it. The result is you don't take your proper turn, give it a wristy hit confined mostly to the hands and, too many times, get off a bad shot which further demoralizes you. *I would say that the biggest problem in hitting the long irons is mostly a mental one. So swing easily and let the club do the job. You'll be surprised—and gratified—at the results.*

PACE YOUR POWER

By Bill Campbell

No top professional would think of swinging as hard as he could all the time and neither should you. *What you should do is swing within yourself for the first few holes.* You can then find out how you are hitting the ball —straight, slicing or hooking—and take any steps necessary to insure hitting it straight before you subject the swing to the strain of an all-out effort. By getting the swing into the groove early, you will be able to let out the shaft successfully when it's necessary—on the long par-fours and par-fives. Many youngsters are especially prone to be "club-conscious" and to belt everything from a drive to a nine-iron as hard as they can. Often they outdrive me on the early holes and are tickled pink. Then on one of the longer holes, where it matters, I send the ball past them. They get so worried they start overhitting everything, their swings collapse, and I've got them. *Sometimes you will find that no matter what you try, your swing won't get into the groove on those early holes. On those days be content to swing within yourself all day.* Using maximum power then is pure folly. *One time when it is helpful to hit all out is toward the end of the match. Pressure is building up and often you are becoming too tired to coordinate properly. I find that hitting hard then actually keeps my swing in the groove.*

THINK HIGH TO HIT HIGH

By Frank Boynton

I am convinced that hitting the ball high is the better way to play. The shot is easier to control, stays in the air longer and has less roll when it lands on the greens. It is an extremely valuable shot to have, and *it isn't too difficult to master once you develop the feeling of swinging a long way through the ball, extending the arc of the swing by going out toward your target with your hands.* It might help to *think* of hitting it high, just as you would if you were to find your ball behind a tree. When faced with this unpleasant prospect, and you decide that you are able to loft a ball up and over, you don't look at the base of the tree, you look up high, well above the trouble, and the chances are that the shot you hit clears the obstacle with plenty of room to spare. It is also similar to driving downwind. Most golfers are better when the wind is behind them because they make more of an effort to hit the ball high and take advantage of the breeze. Use these same tactics to get all your shots a bit higher into the air. *You'll find that by staying behind the shot longer and extending the swing, you can hit the high ball* equally well out of bent grass, clover or off hard ground where you otherwise would risk flying a shot. *And it is an ideal way to hold any green you hit to.*

84

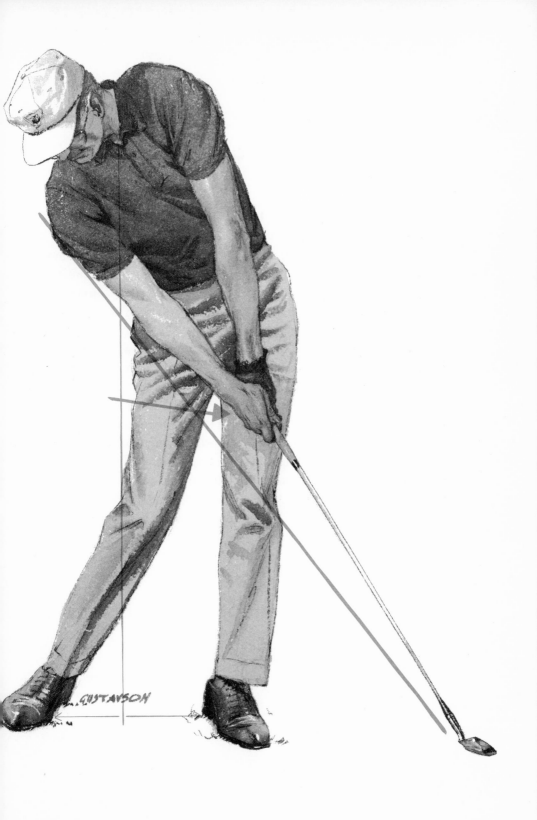

THE FOLLOW–THROUGH

By Dave Ragan

One of the keys to hitting the ball straight, in my opinion, is the proper follow-through. When I swing, one of my major objectives is to make certain I don't roll the wrists over in a counterclockwise motion that causes the clubface to shut after impact. This turning-over motion leads to a hook. I also try to avoid "collapsing" on the follow-through. This is just the reverse of turning over and causes a fade or slice. *After impact I keep the blade as square as I can as long as I can, concentrating on keeping it going toward the hole and keeping it as close to the ground as I can. I find that the straighter I go through the ball, the straighter I hit it.* After impact my arms are fully extended, and as I follow through I keep my right arm in an extended position. My full-arm extension with the club-head has given me a high finish. I don't concentrate on achieving a high finish but find it results from full extension after impact. This complete extension probably causes me to take a larger divot than most of the boys on tour. I play my irons from the center of the stance forward, playing the ball from the center with the nine-iron and moving it a little bit forward as I hit longer shots. On wood shots I play the ball opposite my left heel.

GOLF EXTRA:
TEN WAYS TO KEEP A GOLF
WIDOW HAPPY

By Lester David

What follows herewith could be the best thing for your game since you learned what to do about that slice.

Marital experts are pondering the problem of the golf widow, which has become sizable as the game itself zooms in popularity. They have become aware that while a few million males are daffy about the sport, their wives may take a dim view of having the man of the house away so much. Especially since they are left home with the kids on weekends.

We asked the authorities—marriage counselors, psychologists, family relations experts—if they could come up with some workable advice designed to keep the girls happy, the marriage solid and the golfing male's mind on his shots.

They could and they did.

Make no mistake, though. The institution of golf widowhood may take a lot of joshing, but the problem often can be more serious than a Sid Caesar television skit might indicate. Dr. Harold Kenneth Fink, a Fort Lauderdale psychologist, asserts that marriages can well be wrecked on this reef. Consider, for example, this scene, taken from the files of a marriage counselor:

It's Saturday night, just before bedtime. The man is getting golfing clothes ready for a fast start the following morning. "Again?" says a flat, cold voice. He looks up to see his wife, tight-lipped and flushing. "Why, yes," he says defensively, "didn't you know I was going?"

"You promised the children you would take us to the civic association picnic," she reminds him pointedly. He does remember and his guilt makes him speak out more sharply than he intended: "Oh, for heaven's sake! Are you helpless? Can't you get the Gordons to take you? You know how I feel about golf."

"Yes," she answers in that metallic voice. "I know." She says nothing more, only a cold good night.

"This couple has allowed golf to harm their marriage," asserts Dr. Rebecca Liswood, a nationally prominent marital authority who is executive director of the Marriage Counseling Service of Greater New York. "The man has done little to make his wife feel wanted and important. He is concerned solely with his own golfing enthusiasm. As a result, she feels left out, almost deserted. She is responding to his actions with strong resentment, seeking ways to get back at him.

"A powerful weapon she can use—and indeed is being employed by other women in similar situations—is withholding sex. This, in turn, can trigger hostility on his part and the marriage will be in real trouble."

Let's examine the golf widow more closely. About 30 percent of golfers' wives, according to several estimates, are enthusiastic players themselves and often accompany their husbands to the courses. The rest react to male participation in a wide variety of ways, ranging from approval and amused tolerance to resignation and fury.

Why does she get so all-fired mad? A fascinating answer comes from Dr. Fink, who is especially qualified to talk about sports widows because he has counseled innumerable unhappy wives in Fort Lauderdale, a resort area. They sat in tears in his office, complaining bitterly about their mates who were even at that moment disporting themselves in fishing boats and on the links.

"A woman sees in sports a very distinct rival for her love and affection," Dr. Fink explains. "If a man goes all out for golf or any other sport, devoting large chunks of his time to it, a woman's mind might well flash back to happier days when he was courting her and all this passion and interest were aimed in her direction.

"As a result, she can actually come to hate any symbol of the sport that has, in a very literal sense, stolen her man from her. The very sight of a golf club can send her into a towering rage."

Probe a mite deeper into a woman's psyche. Psychiatrists explain that the way things are in our social setup a woman doesn't control her own destiny. She must rely upon a man for support, for her happiness, for fulfillment of most of her needs.

Knowing she needs a man's protection for herself and her children, knowing too she is emotionally as well as physically dependent upon him, she will fear and resent anything that threatens to remove him, whether it's another woman—or a bagful of golf clubs. If a man lavishes *all* his time and tenderness upon the game, she instinctively fears she is being supplanted and that her security is being threatened.

Then she reacts. Some have been known to retaliate in ways less drastic than sexual coldness but discomfiting nonetheless. Cold meals, for instance. A Long Island woman known to this writer serves her husband canned and only slightly heated hash each time he comes home from a golf session that lasts and lasts. If he's reasonable, he gets a good dinner.

A Chicago woman was less subtle. Her husband promised to spend his vacation at home with her but began playing golf day after day—alone. Burned up when he left for the sixth time in a row, she draped a huge funeral wreath on her front door. Beneath it, she lettered a huge sign: "Golf Widow." He got the point.

A young redhead from Detroit really lowered the boom. She rose before dawn one day and drove home to mother with her two children. In the trunk of the car she had packed all her clothes, the kids' clothes—and his golf clubs. He pleaded two weeks before he got them all back.

Dr. Fink points out that even if a man's marriage isn't really harmed, it's a cinch his golf score will be.

"Few husbands," he asserts, "can rivet their attention on the shots at hand when a voice in the back of their heads keeps telling them that strong dissatisfaction is brewing at home and, in fact, may already have brewed and spilled over. A man is bound to have some guilt feelings which can result in tension and anxiety." And who needs these when you're trying to sink a 12-foot putt?

Well, what's the answer?

On the one hand, golf is one of the most stimulating and gratifying of sports, a challenge and a tonic. But on the other, there are far too many wives who do not look upon the game with the same pleased eye as a

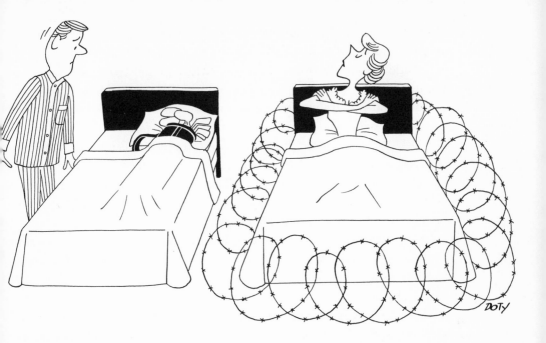

man. How, then, do you keep a golf widow a happy, ever-loving spouse while you go out, with a free mind, knowing you have her encouragement? The answer can help you rack up nice numbers on the score cards. Here are ten suggestions from the experts:

1. *Get her to learn the game herself.*

Convince her, if you can, that the before-mentioned 30 percent of golfers' wives who play themselves have a whale of a time. If you can get her to join this ever-growing sorority, you will accomplish three major goals:

First, you will give her something to do while you're away so that she won't feel left out of things. Second, she will become more sympathetic with your own deep interest in the sport. A golfer can always understand another golfer's problems better than a nonplayer. And third, Dr. Fink points out, you will be able to share another interest with one another and even play together. You'll also have something else to talk about at home. One man whose wife learned to play and became quite good told a New York psychiatrist: "Now we turn off the TV and talk about the shots we made and the ones we missed. Before, we just sat before the box and had little to say except fix me a sandwich. You know, she's a lot more interesting than I thought!"

Dr. Fink tosses in a caution here: It's far wiser not to try to teach her yourself. He explains that husbands are too critical most of the time and lack patience with their own wives. "Some of the most explosive quarrels occur when a man decides he wants to teach his wife to drive a car," he asserts, "and golf isn't much different. Best leave the teaching to a pro."

2. *Keep switching and staggering your playing time.*

Clark W. Blackburn, director of the Family Service Association of America, says: "It could be a depressing thing indeed for a wife to feel that she must look forward to an endless succession of husbandless weekends once the weather turns nice. Her unhappiness and discontent are bound to multiply as the summer wears along.

"To avoid this, a man might try quitting work early now and then on a summer weekday and going directly to the course. Or he may try to get in a round early on a weekday morning, if his work permits. Then the weekend could be left free for the family."

Dr. Liswood tells about the two California attorneys who arrange to meet their wives for dinner after one of their late-afternoon games. "It works fine," she reports. "They get to play, the girls get taken out, the families spend the weekend together—and then nobody minds if the boys go out by themselves the next Sunday."

3. *Give her equal time off.*

Well, enough to make her feel she too can get out into the world once in a while. "The husband who suggests to his wife, 'Why don't you get away for a while this weekend?' is pulling a real masterstroke," explains a Boston marital consultant. "It's great for her and great for him."

Adds Mr. Blackburn, who agrees with the gambit: "Tell her not to worry about things at home, that you will care for the youngsters and watch over all details. Just suggest she take some friends, some money and time."

How can a wife so considerately treated complain if you want to go out with the boys and knock a few balls around?

4. *Convince her of the crucial importance of exercise.*

The New Frontier's "vigah" campaign wasn't just a gimmick. Medical studies have shown conclusively that exercise not only puts more life into your years but adds more years to your life. As proof, quote Dr. Paul Dudley White, the eminent heart specialist who was President Eisenhower's doctor when he suffered his coronary in Colorado in 1955. Dr. White has said that if Ike had not been an ardent golfer most of his adult

92

life, he might have been stricken with his attack ten years sooner! Then, while she's mulling that over, read her this really significant statement made by Dr. White—and incidentally digest it well yourself:

"I believe that the physiological effect of regular exercise throughout one's life will probably, in time, be proved one of the best antidotes against the alarming development of the epidemic of coronary thrombosis and high blood pressure in this country. Along with exercise, of course, there should be recognition of the wisdom of preventing overweight and of avoiding rich food heavy with animal fat."

Suppose she counters with the argument: "Why can't you get your exercise around the house—exercise is exercise, isn't it?"

The answer: It's not! Doctors say that exercise you hate is worse than none at all because it brings on stress. The best kind is what you enjoy —and *you* happen to enjoy golf.

5. *Bring her a box of candy even though it's not Mother's Day.*

Flowers and/or anything from the novelty jewelry counter will do as well—but let's rush to explain that these are not intended as bribes but simply to convince her that she is still important to the guy. The point is worth exploring because it hits close to the heart of things:

A married man, marital authorities explain, doesn't need the reassurance of love words and spontaneous gifts as a woman does, therefore he finds it tough to understand her emotions when they aren't forthcoming. He feels that the old moonglow stuff is behind him, but she doesn't. It's important to her.

"As the years go on," Dr. Liswood asserts, "a wife may begin to feel neglected unless she gets proof that she's important to a man. She wonders if her husband cares as he once did. Anxieties develop as she starts feeling less and less sure of her ground. Then, if her husband begins leaving her alone more and more frequently to woo a golf ball, the fear may become a certainty. She is then a golf widow wearing the blackest of weeds. She feels abandoned, and trouble of all sorts can develop."

A man can prevent this chain of events from occurring by showing his wife that he still values her as a woman. Words, gifts and the romance bit now and then tell her the story she wants to hear—that she's still a wanted wife, not a housekeeper.

The moral: A box of candy can be just as important for your golf game as tipping the caddie.

6. *Plan HER Sunday too.*

Experts agree that one of the worst things a golfer can do is pack his gear, make his plans and push off in the early hours without thought to what the wife is going to do. Especially if he takes the car too and leaves her and the kids stranded in the split-level. Of course, if she's perfectly agreeable because she's got a variety of things she prefers to do, that's fine. But far more often she's left alone with a houseful of boredom. Next stage, discontented golf widowhood. In New York one wife complained: "Not only does he take off every weekend, but he doesn't even bother to get the TV set fixed when it breaks."

Be smart. Before you leave, preferably a day or two in advance, figure out something for her to do too. Would she want to visit her folks? Have company? Get a card game going? Go to a movie or get to a playground with the kids? Make the arrangements. If necessary, work up some sort of car pool deal with neighbors. Do the youngsters want to spend the night at grandma's? Then take them there the evening before. The whole idea is not to leave them all high and dry and lonely while you have fun.

Most important: If it's at all possible, leave the family with some kind of transportation so they can get places if they wish.

7. *Light up an interest for her.*

In Buffalo a department store executive brought home an easel and some oil paints and, without realizing it, solved his own domestic golf problem. In a short time his wife became an enthusiastic amateur painter. "She used to hate to see me leave to play golf," he reported to a friend. "Now she can't wait to get me out of the house so she can get to the studio we fixed up for her in the basement." The point, as Dr. Fink explains, is just this: "If a wife is busy with an activity of her own, she won't be brooding about *your* absence." So look for a spark and light it up. It could be anything—garden clubs, community work, acting with a local group, playing with an amateur symphony, needlepoint—whatever she enjoys doing. If the activity takes her out of the house, you'll need a sitter for the kids, but the investment is more important than green fees.

In Westchester, N. Y., a doctor suggested that his wife reactivate her long-dormant interest in pottery. She formed a clay modeling group which meets regularly in his home while he's on the course. She hardly knows he's gone. In a Boston suburb a once-disconsolate golf widow conducts a current events workshop in her home, come Sundays. Once, when her husband had a fever and couldn't play, *he* sat bored and lonely

94

in his room all afternoon. "I was a current events widower," he lamented.

8. *Don't cut too many classes.*

"If a man plays golf regularly," cautions Mr. Blackburn, "he should not also go bowling with the boys once a week, play poker another time and bring home work from the office two other nights." You might come home one day and the baby will wonder who the stranger might be. Worse, you'll really have a teed-off golf widow on your hands.

9. *Prove to her there's a major social advantage in the game.*

If you can show her that your golf game can move her a notch or two up the social ladder, you've got it made. It's no secret—women are social climbers at heart. That's no knock, by the way. It's in the great American tradition of onward and upward. Now *you* know that you meet plenty of nice guys on the course or at the club, guys who may also be important. But does *she* know? Invite one or two to your home for dinner and show her. You'll be amazed at the added status it will give her—and you too, so far as she is concerned.

There's another sly reason for this. If you can get her to meet, know and like the sort of folks you hobnob with on the course, it won't hurt a bit.

10. *Take a family break.*

Declares Dr. Robert D. Weitz, a New Jersey consulting psychologist: "Even though a man loves golf dearly and wants to play at every opportunity, he must realize he has obligations in his life pattern to his wife and children. So skip a Sunday on the course once in a while and take 'em all out somewhere. Drive to the beach, go on a picnic, visit a museum or maybe just stay home and play ball with the kids. Next week you'll do a lot better with the foursome on the course if you know that the foursome —or fivesome or whatever—at home is on your side.

Toss away whatever amateur means you've been employing on how to handle a golf widow and put these into practice. They're scientifically designed to cure a nagging problem that can affect your score as surely as a bad grip.

III. CHIPPING AND PITCHING
FOR ONE-PUTT

How many strokes would be cut from your score if seventy-five percent of your chip and pitch shots were up for one-putt? I dare say, for most of us, quite a few. Yet few players, outside of the professionals and top amateurs, play these shots well. In the succeeding pages, outstanding pros and a twice National Amateur champ offer sensible advice for getting close to the hole every time.

7. PRO POINTERS ON CHIPPING AND PITCHING

THE CRUCIAL CHIP

By Art Wall, Jr.

If those six-footers are bothering you and perhaps ruining a good game, one solution to the putting problem is better chipping. Any chip shot, if properly hit, should result in a one-putt green. If you leave the ball too far short or knock it past, it stands to reason that those putts won't always drop for you. But good chipping will improve the law of averages. The first thing to remember when chipping is to *be sure that the ball lands on the green*. This provides a more predictable bounce and roll. Usually, I chip with a six-iron when I'm near the edge of the green. I pick a spot on the green where I want my ball to land and then concentrate on hitting that spot. By playing the ball off my right foot with a slightly open stance, my hands will come into the shot well ahead of the clubhead. I try to lead the shot with the back of my left hand and the palm of my right. This makes for a firm stroke and helps to prevent scooping or flipping. *An important point to emphasize in chipping is the grip pressure. I'm very conscious of gripping the club firmly with the last three fingers of the left hand and the thumb and forefinger of the right hand.* Since the "feel" of the shot comes from the hands, a good firm grip is essential to better chipping.

THE PAYOFF CHIP

By Howie Johnson

Chipping to the pin from just off the green calls for pinpoint accuracy, if you'll pardon the pun. It is often the only means of salvaging a par when your approach shot has missed the putting surface. And since you'd like to consider it as your first putt, regardless of the club you've selected to execute this shot, a fine touch is necessary. The key, then, to a successful chip shot is a crisp, solid hit and firm hand action. *I employ a very narrow stance with most of my weight on the left foot, playing the ball just inside the right foot and, with the hands well ahead of the clubhead, catch the ball on the downstroke.* The club, hands and arms all work in unison. I usually set myself up in an open position, about half-facing the hole. This allows my hands to move in front of my body without restriction. I grip down on the club, my right hand being only two to three inches above the steel shaft. At address, the blade of the club is square to the intended line, and I try to remain square throughout the stroke. The normal loft of the club you use to chip with gives the ball the needed trajectory, and the momentum from the stroke will carry the ball up to —and, you hope, into—the hole. The payoff chip spells b-i-r-d-i-e.

100

LET THE CHIPS FLY HIGH

By Don January

Chip shots in wind or rain, or both, require headwork more than any change in one's swing. You must think out the shot carefully, in terms of the weather conditions, and adhere to your advance plan. For instance, take the most frequent conditions of wetness—the early morning with the dew lying heavy or in a steady rain. For the "rain" shot you must, first off, go for more lofted clubs. Go down, let's say, from a normal six-iron to an eight-iron. Shoot right at the hole, because the ball will have little or no run on wet greens. *Play the ball a little forward of your normal chip position to get added loft, but don't change your stance, swing or style of hitting. Remember, loft is obtained by moving the position of the ball slightly ahead of normal, a little more toward the line of the left heel.* It is just the opposite downwind with no rain. Here you must figure on letting the wind do some of the work, again going for loft. *On a 20-yard pitch, for instance, 20 feet of it should be given to the wind.* Above all, though, remember to use your head before stepping up to hit in wind and rain!

THE SAFETY SHORT GAME

By Charlie Coe

The best suggestion for any amateur golfer who's interested in reducing his score is to play the safety short game—and give it plenty of practice. *Amateurs on the whole don't practice those short chips and pitch shots anywhere near enough.* You'll see them on the putting green or hitting a few shots with their woods before they tee off, but they go out cold with an even colder short game. *When I say the safety short game, I mean take a club with more loft than you think you need, particularly if you don't play very often.* There probably are more flubbed four-iron shots on little chips around the green than anything else. That's because the player is *trying to lift the ball. Instead of taking the risky four-iron, use a nine-iron, hit down on it and the ball has got to get up, leaving you less margin of error.* In playing this shot, keep the hands well ahead of the club face. The arms have to move some, of course, but this is primarily a wrist shot. The next time you see the pros, notice how they play these short shots from off the green, and how they position their hands ahead of the ball —and keep them there. That's why they chip so close to the cup so often. *But even if you can't devote enough time to practice, try keeping the hands ahead on those short chips. Use more loft, hit down on the ball and you should soon be giving your opponents cause for real concern around the green.*

THE PITCH SHOT

By Jacky Cupit

One of the most helpful things I have learned on tour is how to hit the high-soft pitch and the low-running pitch. The fellow who taught me these shots is Lionel Hebert, one of the best teachers in golf. The lofted pitch is a "must" when you must hit over a trap or other hazard and get the ball to sit down quickly. This type of shot is especially necessary when the pin is set close to a trap or when the green is hard. *Here's how to hit this delicate shot: open the blade of the pitching wedge and your stance slightly. Move the left hand counterclockwise on the shaft until the "V" formed by the thumb and forefinger points toward the left shoulder. This is known as a very weak left-hand grip. Hit the shot, using this grip.* You'll find the ball will go higher and sit down faster. *To execute the low-running shot, do just the opposite in taking the grip with the left hand. In other words, assume a very strong left-hand grip.* In hitting the low-running pitch, I play the ball back in my stance to insure low trajectory.

THE POPCORN SHOT

By Joe Stoddard

Here is a challenge that will cut strokes off your game when mastered, but will add a few if you insist on trying it on the course prematurely or carelessly. It is, or can be, highly effective from the immediate vicinity of the green. The popcorn shot, so called because the stroke will pop the ball up and onto the putting surface with little run, can get you out of any lie on dirt or grass. It is actually a cut shot, played from an open stance with the face of the wedge also open. If the lie is tight, play the ball off the left foot to give the clubhead enough room to hit the ball and the ground almost simultaneously. If on soft grass, which offers some "give," move it back just a little: Balance must be maintained. To pop the ball up, you will have to hit down. *Without shifting any weight to the right side, take the club back slightly outside the line, with an immediate wrist break. From this point keep the wrists firm, then, with a two-handed effort, swing through the ball. The actual pull is with the left hand, which must at all times stay ahead of the right. Pressure is felt on the lower three fingers of the left, your weight is back, and the downswing arc stays unbroken as the clubhead goes through the ball.* It is similar to a trap shot, except the release is less, that is, the body remains solidly in place. The higher the shot, the more upright the backswing. Because the ball will spin to the right, aim to the left of the pin. Hit the back of the ball, remember to follow through and it will pop up.

WEDGE SHOTS CAN BE FUN

By Joe Campbell

The short pitch to the flag from the fairway with a wedge is a most satisfying shot—and fun. This is the shot played from a few feet to about 30 yards from off the putting surface. The ball must have some grass under it, so that the club can get under the ball and lob it into the air. *I repeat, don't attempt this shot off any sort of a bare or tight lie. Otherwise, the flange of either wedge is liable to skull the ball, which will tend to take the fun out of the shot!* I play this shot with my feet quite close together, with a slightly open stance. I relax my grip a little, because this is not a "power" shot—it is to be played softly, almost lovingly. *I start the clubhead back under sensitive control of the hands, breaking my wrists a little sooner than on a normal shot, and start back to the ball slowly. At impact, the clubhead is under the ball.* Follow through normally. I would point out that you need not make any effort to create backspin. You will find that the club will provide all the stop you require. The ball will go slowly up into the air and, when it hits the green, it lands as light as a feather. After a bounce or two, it will roll very little. Try it sometime —you'll enjoy it.

GOLF EXTRA:
HOW TO WIN MATCHES

By Harry Obitz and Dick Farley

Confidence and bold playing win matches. To gain confidence, it is essential to have and follow a plan of action. Think out the course you're going to play beforehand and decide such things as where you will go strong off the tee and where you will just keep the ball in play. Having devised your plan, don't deviate from it unless, of course, it means losing the hole.

Now that you have a plan of attack thought out, let's consider the match itself. Here are our ten golden rules for success:

1. Know your own game. Never count on doing better than your average. You will have some good holes and some bad holes. Your opponent will, too. This sort of thinking will keep you from blowing up when things go wrong or being too elated when they are right.

2. Study the course conditions—they will radically affect your play. On a dry course play run-up shots. On a wet day play pitch shots right to the hole. On a windy day you again want to play low, bouncing shots. Remember that the speed of the greens can change during the day. In the early morning the dew will make them slow. In the afternoon, when the sun has dried them out, they will be faster.

3. Play the shot you know you can make—not a fancy shot out of a book.

4. Study your opponent's style during the first few holes. It can often give you a lot of confidence! A player with several faults will surely come ungrooved before the end.

5. Play your game shot by shot, and don't worry about your bad shots. Remember that a bad shot in match play can, at worst, mean *one* lost hole. Never give up on a hole and waste strokes. In singles many a hole is won with a bogey.

6. Play position with *every* shot. Always plan one shot *ahead* to make your next shot easier.

7. Try to hole everything from 30 yards in. Not that you *will* hole all

112

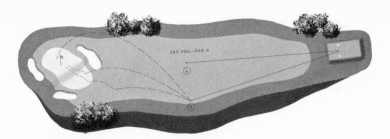

Player A walked straight onto the tee and hit right down the middle—into a bad position. If A's second is long or short, he's in a trap. If he's too far to the left, he stays down on the bottom plateau of the green. Only a perfect shot will hit on the top and stop. If the green weren't holding, A couldn't get close. Player B noticed the tee was not squared with the best line for the drive, so he hit out to the left. B has three shots he can play: he can hit to the top level, pitch and run, or run it up.

Always consider course conditions before selecting your club. Never just pull out the regular club you use for the shot, without giving it a thought. Here, A did just that. He took his nine-iron, up it went in the air, the wind was blowing against so the ball fell short and in the lake. B took a straighter-faced club than normal and played a pitch-and-run close.

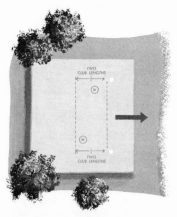

Intelligent use of the full teeing area can mean playing off a level rather than an uneven lie. By using the width (A) and depth (B) of a tee, you may even avoid going over a trap on a par-three. Avoid teeing up in a mess of divots; they can make you play down the line they're pointing and most of them point the wrong way.

of them, but because this positive attitude will leave you closer to the hole than a wishy-washy effort. Once in a while, one will drop and really shake your opponent.

8. Play *away* from trouble. We know this sounds obvious, but so many players will dispatch a beautiful drive straight into a fairway bunker, when with a little care they could have been in good shape.

9. Always play at your own pace. If you usually play slowly, don't allow your opponent to speed up the game and throw you off your normal pace. If you normally play fast and your opponent is playing slowly, keep yourself in motion by walking forward and studying your next shot some more.

10. Don't let up when you are ahead. This is *fatal.* Keep playing each hole according to your plan.

Now, when it comes to playing a four-ball, you and your partner should start from the first tee with the idea of playing for birdies. A slow start can be very costly, because in this type of match it mostly takes a birdie to *win* a hole. Holes are very seldom won with pars. Also, at the

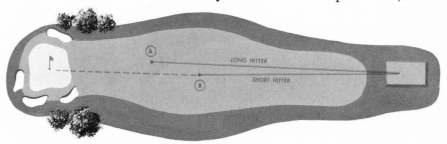

Never try to match a long hitter. Drive, if anything, a little more within yourself, because this way you get to shoot first at the green. If you hit a good one, as B did, you will really shake your opponent. The long hitter, A, now has a lot of pressure on him.

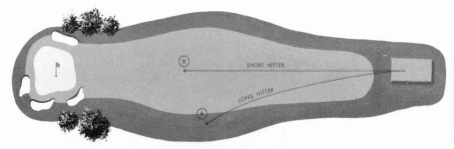

When the long hitter knocks one into the brush as A did, that's the time for short hitter, B, to let out the shaft and try and out hit him. Long hitters hate to be out-driven. It hurts their pride—and often their second shots.

114

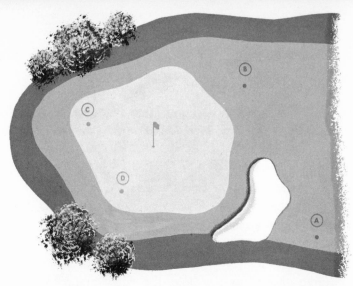

Opponents C and D are on the green in regulation figures. A and B both missed it in regulation. A has a bunker to play over, but B has an open shot. Though A is away, B can and should play first, because he has the best chance of shooting close. If he does, this will give A greater confidence and he, too, will probably make a good shot. This way C and D face two balls close to the hole and the pressure is on them. Had A played first and flubbed the shot, the pressure would have been on B. Meanwhile C and D would have stood by watching A and B making a mess of it. You can apply this idea on approach shots of any distance when your side is away.

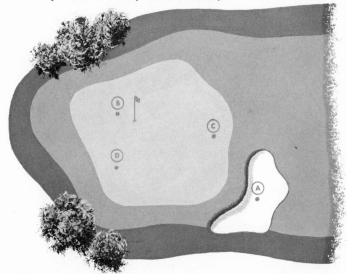

C and D are on the green in regulation figures, both about 15 feet away. B is five feet away, putting for a birdie, while A missed the green in regulation and is in the trap. B should putt out first. If he gets it, A can't improve, but A and B have put the pressure on C and D—one of them has to sink a 15-footer. If B misses, he still makes a par and A gets a chance at an all-or-nothing shot for the birdie from the bunker, before C or D get a chance to try for their birdies. If A had shot first and put his ball onto the green inside C and D, then A and B would have forfeited the option and allowed C and D two cracks at a birdie, before B had the opportunity to sink his. If either C or D got the birdie, then B's putt would have seemed a mile long.

start elect a captain for the side—usually the player with more experience. It is this player's job to make the tactical decisions.

To cover every situation in four-ball play would require a book in itself. We will zero in on those points that many players overlook. In essence, all the hints we could give you add up to two golden rules:

1. Give your partner confidence.
2. Give your opponents fits!

All other considerations flow from these two.

On par-threes the better iron player should shoot first. Having the accurate iron player already on the green can give the weaker iron shooter confidence. If you have the honor, this puts the pressure on your opponents.

Before teeing off on *any* key hole, the side's strategy should be discussed and decided. Of course, the state of the match will sometimes reverse your original plans for any key hole.

One of the things amateurs forget is that if your side is away *either* of you can shoot next. Don't confine your use of this option to the putting green. It can work in your favor on *any* approach shot, or even on seconds on par-fives.

Remember, the idea is to give your partner confidence. So, when your side is away, *the player with the best chance of making the shot should play first*. A successful shot on his part will encourage his partner to make a success of the more difficult shot. And two successful shots can really put the pressure on your opponents.

While we're on this subject of options, there may be times when you prefer not to surrender the option. By this we mean have the player who is nearer the hole play first—*regardless of the difficulty of the shot*. The thinking here is to get two shots near the hole before your opponents have the chance to match your shots.

Where options and the matter of giving confidence to your partner conflict, each case will have to be decided on its merits. But always think about the situation before making a decision. A clear plan can give each partner a better picture of what he has got to do and increases his chances of making a successful shot.

Confidence will not come from ignorance, but will be fostered by planned knowledge. Playing bold does not mean playing with the blinders on, but rather knowing what you must do and then doing it!

On holes where a gamble can set up a birdie, the longer hitter, A, should go first, because he has a better chance of cutting the dogleg. If A succeeds, then B, the shorter hitter, can also gamble a little. If A gets into trouble, then B plays a safe shot to the center of the fairway.

On a hole like this, it might be well for both partners to hit into position on the flat part of the fairway, "A," the longer hitter, hitting a two-iron, "B" hitting a three-wood. A slice means rough or out-of-bounds. A hook means the quarry. A second shot from the rough anywhere on this hole is not inviting.

IV.   PLAYING FROM THE SAND

In the years since the sand wedge was developed, the techniques of playing sand shots have become quite standard and surprisingly easy to follow. Yet for some unknown reason, the weekend player misses more sand shots than he should. In the following pages, you'll find sand shot demonstrations from a number of the finest sand players in the world, so clearly explained that hereafter the sand trap should trouble no one.

8.   FOOLPROOF SAND SHOTS

By Julius Boros

It was steaming, sizzling, smoking hot in Dallas in June 1952, and so was my sand wedge. It was one of the major reasons why I won the United States Open that year and also 11 years later in 1963.

I've always felt that the sand wedge is the most overlooked club in the bag. Hit all your other clubs perfectly and you probably won't need that sand wedge, but none of us ever manage to hit all flawless shots. Somewhere, sometime, you're going to be in the sand and you'd better know exactly how to get out—not only know how to pop it flush off the sand, but to explode it up there close enough to get your birdie or salvage your par.

But back to Dallas. Ben Hogan is an awful feller to have breathin' down your neck. Even today, most of us would hate to have him giving you that razor-blade stare if you were all even and going to the last hole head and head. At Dallas I wasn't what you'd call a case-hardened playing professional. Sure, I'd won the Massachusetts Open in 1951. Yet only two years earlier, I'd been beaten in the quarter-finals of the U.S. Amateur. So here I was, in 1952, leading in the final round of the U.S. Open. At a time like this you look over your shoulder, no matter how easygoing and phlegmatic people might think you are, and you feel the goose pimples marching up and down your back. You give them the old poker face and the unhurried appearance of nonchalance, but, I have to admit, you know this isn't an ordinary round of golf. Not with guys like Hogan and the late Porky Oliver staring down the gun barrel at you.

By the time I came to the thirteenth hole, with Hogan about five holes behind me, I had a two-stroke lead. On the thirteenth I caught a trap. Out came the sand wedge. I popped it four feet from the hole and ran it down for a birdie that put me three shots in front. On the next hole, the fourteenth, a 490-yard par-five, I knocked my one-iron second shot clean over the green into a shallow trap in the rear of the green. Fortunately I had a good lie. Again I used the sand wedge and this time knocked it two inches from the hole. I tapped the ball in for the second straight birdie and a four-stroke lead. That's the exact number of shots by which I won my first Open championship. It sure does sound easy when you talk about it a dozen years later.

But let me drive home my point right here. If I hadn't practiced for my master's degree with the sand wedge, I couldn't possibly have won. There are many fine wedge players in this game of golf and none of them got there the easy way.

Sure, I can tell you how you should play it, and a little practice will give you an edge. But keep in mind that a lot of practice is the only sure way in which you can be certain that the wedge will pop it off the sand and make the cup say uncle.

The basic rules you should bear in mind are:
1. Have the blade open at address.
2. Hit from one to two inches behind the ball.
3. Swing smoothly and easily.
4. Follow through fully.

There are, of course, slight variations, which I will get to later. But these are the keys to playing a trap shot around the green when you have a respectable lie.

I play this type of a shot with an open stance, the feet being slightly farther apart than in chipping. The stance also turns the shoulders toward the green, permitting a free follow-through. The ball is played about two inches inside the left heel with the feet well planted in the sand. Generally speaking, your backswing for the desired distance should be just a little longer than for a pitch shot of the same distance.

Let me caution you right here not to try to scoop the ball off the sand. If you do, you'll probably hit halfway up the ball and skull it right over the green.

There are two other types of explosion shots which you will come up against from time to time.

One is when the sand in the trap is wet. In this case, I play a half-blast shot. I use a shorter swing than usual and take a little less sand.

The other is when you haven't had any rain, the sand is exceptionally dry and your ball buries itself. Two alterations are made in such a case. First, you must close the face of the club slightly. Second, you must hit as much as three inches behind the ball.

The reason you close the face is to take maximum advantage of the

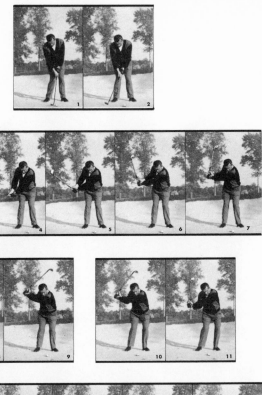

For the sand shot, Boros addresses the ball with the clubface slightly open and the hands ahead of the ball. The club is picked up with a quick breaking of the wrists, which become fully cocked before the top of the swing. A three-quarter swing is used, and there is a fluid change of direction from the top of the swing to the start of the downswing. Hands lead the club into the hitting area. The clubhead enters the sand well behind the ball, exploding it out. Once contact with the sand is made, the right hand begins to turn over the shaft. Note the full follow-through.

force of the clubhead. Closing the face assures you of a more pronounced explosion. Hitting farther behind the ball ensures that the clubhead will dig in and blast the ball out of the depression it is in. You still must

When you face this lie with the ball below you in the trap, flex your knees a little more and hold the club at the end of the grip to make sure you get down to the ball.

swing all the way through, however, to be certain that the ball carries out of the bunker.

One of the most difficult trap shots is when the ball is below the level of the feet, which generally is the case when the ball is in the sand and the feet are on the bank of the trap. Here you require an exaggerated knee bend to get the hands into hitting position. The club is held on the end of the grip and, to maintain balance, I shorten the backswing. The reason for this is that the more body movement, the more you are likely to miss the shot.

Another demanding trap shot is one where you want to carry the ball some distance, say 20-30 yards. The problem here is judging how much sand to take. As a general rule, the longer the shot, the less sand you take and vice versa. Square up the blade, consciously keep more weight on the left side than on the shorter bunker shot, and take a three-quarter

Don't restrict the use of the sand iron to traps. The pros use the sand wedge from heavy rough with great effectiveness.

swing. Try very hard not to *lean forward or backward or sway* during the swing. Because you're taking a fuller swing, you are apt to slide around in the sand. This could cause a skull or, worse, leave the ball in the trap. Don't stop the clubhead at impact as this can be disastrous. Swing down and through to a high finish.

I can't overemphasize the importance of digging in well with your feet as you take your stance. Not only do you get a firm footing, but you can get a good idea of the texture of the sand.

When you are playing out of powdery or "beach" sand, composed of rather fine particles, you can get good action (backspin) on the ball. Hit the sand about an inch behind the ball.

125

Coarse, gravelly sand demands different treatment. Hit closer to the ball, and expect the ball to have a certain amount of run. The reason for this is that the clubface never gets close enough to the ball to put any action on it.

Sometimes, when you're placing your feet in the sand, you will find a layer of hard-packed sand, clay or dirt below the top layer of sand. In this case, there is a danger that the wide flange of the sand wedge will "bounce" off the hard layer, causing a skulled shot. In this case, switch to a pitching wedge or even a nine-iron.

Curiously enough, you should read the greens even when blasting from a trap. For example, if the green runs down and away from you, allow for some roll. The slope takes much of the bite off the ball. If the green slopes upward, carry the ball as close to the pin as possible. The ball will not only hold the green, it's liable to back up on you.

Right and left breaks on a green should also be considered. On left-to-right breaks, remember that the normal spin on the ball will make it "kick" to the right, so play the shot more left than usual. On a right-to-left break, the slope will diminish the amount of spin to the right.

Don't ignore the sand wedge when you're playing off the grass, as this shot is used extensively by the touring professionals. You can get the ball up quickly and it hits the green lightly with little run. The pitching wedge, however, only takes the bite on the second or third hop.

When you are in rough close to the green, play the "pop" shot. Lightly drop the clubhead into the ball, stopping the stroke at impact. This will "jump" the ball out with a minimum of run.

One of the great dangers of trap play is trying to pick the ball clean. I repeat, this can result in flying the ball over the green. An example of just how disastrous this can be occurred in the 1952 World Championship at Chicago's Tam O'Shanter. Going to the sixteenth tee, Patty Berg was within one stroke of tying Betty Jameson for the lead.

The sixteenth is a tough, long par-three hole that carries down across a creek to a well-trapped green. Patty knocked her tee shot into the trap to the right of the green. The pin was directly behind the bunker. It was a tough shot but, to save her par and stay in the race, Patty had to pop the ball up fast and stop it close to the pin for one putt.

Patty tried to explode the ball. But instead she caught it clean, and it sailed clear across the green, stopping in the opposite rough and against a tree. She played a left-handed shot away from the tree, needed another

126

shot to reach the green, and took two putts to get down for a killing six on this par-three hole.

Patty is regarded as one of the finest trap players in the game. But at this vital point her concentration slipped.

So keep your mind on what you're doing and, as Patty will tell you, be sure to take sand with that explosion shot. Open the clubface, hit one to two inches behind the ball and *follow* through. You'll discover that trap shots hold no terrors.

9. PRO POINTERS ON SAND SHOTS

HITTING FROM WET SAND

By Chi Chi Rodriguez

I am well qualified to talk about the explosion shot from wet, packed sand, because in Puerto Rico where I come from we get a lot of rain squalls. On this shot you should address the ball with the clubface wide open, with the bottom edge of the club *facing directly at the hole, not to the left.* You won't put much side spin onto the ball off wet sand and, if the sand is wet, then the green is likely to be wet. *The wet grass* will tend to nullify any side-spin action when the ball hits the green. You should take your normal grip, with both hands in their regular position at the end of the handle. *There's no need to choke up on this shot, so don't do it.* Your stance should be wide open. *The big difference between the way I play a normal trap shot and the one from wet, packed sand is that I hit closer to the ball and don't swing as hard. Normally, I hit one and a half inches behind the ball. On this shot I aim for the sand half an inch behind the ball.* The reason for this is that if I swung as for a normal trap shot and hit the sand where I normally do, *I would run the risk of the flange on the wedge bouncing off the hard, wet sand and skulling the shot.* As you can't vary too much the distance you hit behind the ball safely, the rule should be: the longer the shot, the longer the backswing.

WET SAND

NORMAL SAND

SQUARE TO THE LINE
BUT OPENED FACE

THE RUNNING SAND SHOT

By Bernie Haas

Golf offers many "in-between" situations that are difficult to master in practice and much tougher to execute under pressure. A crucial and interesting problem is the shot from the sand that must travel some 50 to 60 feet to the pin. The problem is further compounded if the green has two levels. There is no doubt that a ball which is knocked out of a sand trap, hits near the hole and spins to a stop is a magnificent shot. However, the art of doing this well all the time is confined to the golfer who plays and practices all the time. Yet even for the seasoned player, the distance sometimes prohibits this method. A more effective way, especially for the less proficient, is *to hit a trap shot that produces roll.* Instead of an open clubface and an open stance, *address the ball nearly square. Swing full but without force, hit three to four inches behind the ball, and the clubhead speed will pop the ball out of the sand, onto the green, to roll some ten to fifteen feet to the pin.* It is a much easier shot to master than the delicate shot with backspin, and under the circumstances the more sensible one.

THE TRAP SHOT

By Bobby Nichols

No shot poses a greater problem for the average player than the sand shot. And, conversely, trap shots don't provide too much trouble for the expert player. I have even heard some players on tour say they'd rather be in a certain trap than in a certain spot on the edge of the green. You'll have more success with trap shots if you follow these hints. (1) When hitting a trap shot, assume the same position as when hitting any other shot of comparable distance. (2) Open your stance slightly with the left hip pointing to the left of the target. (3) Make certain that your feet are firm. (4) As you address the ball open the face of the sand iron slightly. (5) Aim one to two inches behind the ball. (6) *When you take the club back, cock your wrists sooner than on other shots. This gives you the feeling of picking the club up more abruptly on the backswing. It also enables you to hit down into the sand more effectively. The flange of the sand iron will prevent the club from sticking into the sand.* (7) Start the club down as in other shots, making sure the hands lead the clubhead through the shot. Be careful not to let the hands turn or cross over. (8) This shot requires courage. You must be determined not to quit on it but to follow through. It is important that this shot be played with the sand iron, not the pitching wedge. The flange on the sand iron is designed to cause the clubhead to skid through the sand and lift the ball out.

THE ROUGH SHOT FROM THE SAND

By Huston LaClair, Jr.

The sandy lie in the rough, a situation that threatens golfers who play seaside courses, does not mean a stroke has to be wasted just to get the ball back out onto the fairway. It does, however, mean the swing will be slightly different. *Unlike grassy rough, where the ball sits up on roots that offer little or no resistance to the clubhead, the ball in sandy rough is tight, with no room for the club to cut underneath it, and sand has less give.* This calls for hitting the ball first and swinging the club through after impact. You cannot afford to stop or chop or hit on the ball too high or low. *Firm up your stance, especially if the sand is too loose to hold your weight. Never try to hit the ball hard, because you can be thrown off balance. Select a club longer than normal to allow you to reduce your backswing and still get distance, and grip the club a bit tighter in the left hand. The sand doesn't give the way grass does, and a firm, left-hand grip is necessary to keep the clubhead from stopping or turning. Take the club back a little more abruptly, play the ball back to center to insure your hitting it first, then hit it squarely on the nose.* Keep the clubhead going through and you'll burn the ball out of the tight lie, with plenty of distance and good action.

RECOVERING FROM BURIED LIES

By Ed Furgol

One of the most frustrating trouble shots of the game presents itself when a ball becomes buried in the sand. I can say from experience that even tournament players are greatly upset by it. When confronted by a buried lie, most golfers will reach for a sand iron, the club best suited for sand under normal conditions. But when a ball is buried, a sand iron can produce drastic results, such as a skulled shot—one in which the ball whizzes over the green in line-drive fashion—or a dinky pop shot that leaves the balls in the trap. *The correct club to use when confronted by a buried lie is one with a sharp blade, such as a pitching wedge or a nine-iron. The sand iron is a poor choice, because it has a flange or blunt edge that prevents the clubhead from going down far enough for an adequate recovery.* Now the way to use a nine-iron or pitching wedge most effectively when hitting from a buried lie is to play the ball opposite the right foot and swing the club with face closed and in a chopping motion. This enables the clubhead to get below the ball so that it comes out of the trap more accurately and softly.

TRAP SHOT PRECISION

By Bruce Crampton

Often you will see a player try to blast out of a bunker with a nine-iron or pitching wedge, expecting to get good results. He probably won't, even if he plays the shot correctly, because he's using the wrong club. A knowing player will use the precise club made for the job—the sand wedge. This club is heavy, has a lot of loft and a broad sole. It is the back edge of this sole, which strikes the sand first and prevents the club from cutting deeply into the sand, that gives this club the big advantage over the nine-iron or pitching wedge. Where these clubs sink into the sand and tend to muffle the shot, the sand iron bounces or throws the ball out of the trap. So when you take up the sand wedge, remember these basic points: *Play the ball well forward—off your left toe. Take an open stance. Open the clubface. Take the club sharply back and up, outside the line of flight. Stay down on the shot and hit the sand with the back edge of the sole, usually about an inch and a half behind the ball. Be sure to follow through so that the loft of the clubface throws the ball out of the bunker.*

BUNKERING OUT

By Max Faulkner

In hitting an ordinary trap shot, try to imagine you're scooping the ball out with a frying pan. *In addressing the ball, have your stomach almost facing the hole.* This means, of course that the left foot is drawn well back from the line of flight. In other words, employ a very open stance, and be sure it is a wide stance. *Hit about an inch and a half behind the ball. The action will be across the ball. The result will be a cut shot. Because of the cutting action, the ball will bounce to the right. Therefore, be sure to aim the ball about a yard to the left of the pin.* I hit this shot with the ball opposite my left heel. Now, *if the ball is buried, assume a square stance with the feet paralleling the line of flight.* Pick up the club more abruptly on the backswing, hit about one inch behind the ball, dig the ball out and follow through only three or four inches. Take a full backswing and swing as hard as you would if you were hitting a drive. Play the ball past center and almost opposite the right foot so you'll catch it on the downstroke. The ball is bound to come out and when it does it won't have any backspin on it, so allow for a little extra run.

GOLF EXTRA:
WHAT MAKES A GOOD
SENIOR GOLFER?

By Gene Sarazen

It's not so surprising to me that many of our senior pros today are playing so well. The benefit of a sound swing and a conscious awareness of daily health can permit you to play well your entire life. Snead and Hogan, who are of course standouts, are living proof of what a sound swing can do for you, regardless of age. I don't mean to say that we're all as gifted as a Snead or a Hogan, but we all can learn and take advantage of why they still score so well, even though they're not getting any younger.

One noticeable factor in both Snead's and Hogan's games is they both get tremendous distance off the tees without "tearing" at the ball. If the years are taking their toll off the tees, don't compensate for loss of distance by hitting harder—this just magnifies the problem. Work at retaining your timing. Though it has been said before, make the club-head work for you.

As you get older, it becomes harder to hold on to your timing. You've got to be acutely aware of saving everything for the bottom of the swing. When you're young, the swing "happens" automatically, but as the years pile on, I suggest slowing it down a little—especially at the top of the swing. Even if you feel like you're hesitating a bit at the top, this is closer to what you're looking for to produce good timing.

One change that I noticed about my game is that my swing started to become more upright. The reason for this, I found, was a restricted turn. As you get older, it becomes increasingly difficult to take a big pivot into your backswing. The result is the club is brought straight back and up. Therefore, if you don't turn, then you will not take the club toward the inside, and get the proper inside-out swing.

One difficulty in turning stems from that "spare tire" that mysteriously accumulates around the middle every year. My advice in this situation is to stand in front of a full-length mirror and take your stance for hitting

142

a tee shot. Place your hands on your hips and practice turning.

The next step in combating the years is to play as much as possible. Dutch Harrison, who seems to ignore the fact he is a senior citizen, plays as well now as he ever did.

Dutch Harrison believes constant play rather than constant practice is the key for seniors.

The "Arkansas Traveller" feels that *playing* as much as possible is the best thing in the world for your game. As simple as this sounds, there's a good deal of wisdom in this statement. Dutch is against a senior player's "beating his brains out" on the practice tee, when playing a round of golf is so much better for you. Not only does playing help you keep the "touch" and "feel" so necessary to good scoring, but it will stimulate your interest and desire and keep you competitively sharp.

While the luxury of hitting hundreds of balls on the practice tee is for the young who are trying to build up a sound swing, however, I don't recommend that you step out onto the first tee cold. In warming up, start by hitting a few seven-irons and get the rhythm and timing of your swing going. Finish off this part of your warmup with a couple of tee shots. Then go over to the practice green and try some pitches, and finally, work down to your chipping and putting.

In sharpening the short game, remember that another place where age interferes somewhat is in your ability to pitch the ball. I used to take my pitching wedge and fly it right at the flag, and have all the confidence in the world that it would sit right where it landed. But I've found my hands don't control the pitching wedge as well as they once did—I just don't seem to have the hand action necessary for good bite any more.

I know that I'm not alone in this, so I strongly suggest the mastering of the "pitch-and-run" shot. Instead of using the pitching wedge, take a nine-iron or even a seven or eight, depending on the situation, hit the ball a little easier than the wedge, and allow for 15 or 20 feet of run. I'm sure you'll be pleased with the results.

Getting back to our senior pros, I would say the ones who are winning are those professionals who still work and teach at clubs and therefore have a club in their hands all the time.

Now I hear a lot of you saying, "I still have to earn a living. I can't play every day of the week." Well, I will let you in on a small secret. Neither can I! But I do have one swing recipe for keeping your swing young and healthy that has, I think, been responsible for much of the success I've had in recent years.

Gene Sarazen demonstrating how a senior golfer can ignore foul weather and stiff them to the pin with a pitch-and-run shot.

I swing a 22-ounce driver when I'm not playing. I find this keeps my hands and wrists strong and in tune. If you don't have a training club, use your sand wedge. It's short—and so can be swung indoors with little risk to your ceiling—and has plenty of head weight.

I don't play nearly as much as I used to, but keeping the hands and golfing muscles in shape helps immensely in maintaining timing and clubhead feel. Not a day goes by but that I swing my heavy driver. So take a leaf from the Old Squire's book and keep swinging—every day.

V. PUTTING FOR RESULTS

As the purses of the professional tournaments leap to astronomical heights, the putter becomes more and more the prize weapon of the golf world. Not surprisingly, with all that money around, the putting of the professionals gets better and better every year. In the ensuing pages, putters of the caliber of Billy Casper, Art Wall and Paul Harney show you how to solve many of your problems on the green.

10.   HOW TO AVOID THREE-PUTTING

By Harry Obitz and Dick Farley

The average club golfer takes approximately 38–42 putts per round. Against a regulation 36 putts for 18 holes, this means he is taking at least *two to six three-putt greens* a round. A good professional, on the other hand, is taking two or three less than regulation. To *win* a tournament on the PGA tour today you would probably have to *average* around 30 putts a round.

How come the massive difference between the club golfer's performance and that of the tournament winner? Confidence? Practice? Natural ability? Yes, all these are factors in the development of a successful putter. But what about those players who practice their putting from dawn till dark, yet can't buy a putt? We submit their problem is that they have no real *system* of putting. They practice and practice in vain!

A system of putting will build up your confidence and, what's more

Don't visualize your putt as a wafer-thin line.

important, can rebuild your confidence if you temporarily lose your touch.

The first essential to consistent putting takes place before you ever set the blade behind the ball. We mean the matter of "lining up" the putt.

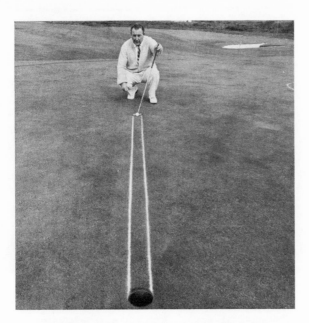

Think of putting along a track to the hole.

This expression has probably caused more missed putts than any other. No, we don't mean you should step up to the putt without figuring such things as break, grain and speed. It's that word "line" that bothers us.

Most weekenders pick out the "line" to the hole, set the putter blade down at right angles to the "line," then try to send the put down this "line" to the hole. Now a *line* is wafer-thin and the poor golfer imagines that if he deviates a fraction of an inch to right or left, he won't hole the putt. In his anxiety to keep his putt straight, he often tenses up, fails to stroke the putt properly—and misses the putt. Yes, that word "line" can scare a golfer more on a putt than if he were asked to tread a high wire over Niagara Falls!

Instead of a line, we suggest you think of putting along a "track" to the hole. This track will be four and a quarter inches wide running from the sides of the hole to the toe and heel of the putter.

First, get down behind the ball and figure out the direction and speed

149

of the putt. Then, set the putter down at right angles to the direction of the putt, and site from the toe of the putter to the right side of the hole and from the heel, to the left side of the hole. This will create in your

Most putters are the same width (heel to toe) as the hole.

mind the image of the four-and-a-quarter-inch track, because the putter blade is usually the same width (heel to toe) as the hole is wide.

Putting down the track will give you confidence, as, in making the stroke, it will seem easy to keep the ball between the two lines. At least, it's a lot easier than putting down one line. That we promise you!

After many years of practicing this "track" method of visualizing the path of the putt, we can get an image of the track in our minds on even the longest, most breaking putt.

At first, you may find it difficult to visualize the track on any putt. In which case, we recommend you start on six- to eight-foot putts and work your way out from the hole. After a while, you'll have little difficulty picturing the track on even the medium putts of, say, 15–20 feet. If, however hard you try, you still cannot "see" the track on long putts all the way to hole, give up! Just select the path you want to hit the putt on, visualize the track for *the first eight feet or so* to the pin and let her fly.

One last thought about the track method of visualizing the putt. Try and develop your own way of "seeing" it. Some players, like ourselves,

150

favor the image conjured up by the word "track." Others find the word "path" more helpful. Still others like to putt down a "trough" or imagine walls on either side of the track, which will prevent the ball going off line.

Putting all four balls in from 18 inches and then from three feet builds up confidence in your ability to hole any putt within the six-foot circle. Repeating this three times reinforces confidence.

We had one player at our club who preferred to "color" the track gold. But then he did win quite a few Nassaus with this method! But whatever you do, never think of a "line" on a putt again!

Now a putting practice routine is another essential to become a confident and, therefore, successful putter. Just aimlessly "practicing" putts is going to get you nowhere. Here's a method we have found very satisfactory.

Make or visualize a circle around the hole six feet in diameter. (Place your putter head in the hole and the other end will lie on the circumference of the circle.) Take four balls and scatter them around the hole about 18 inches away. Now putt them all into the hole. If you miss one, start over again until you hole all four in succession.

Next, place the balls at random at the edge of the circle and putt them in. Again, if you miss one, start over again. This procedure builds up your confidence to hole any short, but missable, putt. When you can go through this routine three times without missing a ball, you'll be ready to practice the longer putts.

151

Go back to 20 feet or beyond and again scatter the balls at random. Now step up and hit each ball, just concentrating on hitting it into the six-foot circle. The reasoning behind this is that once you can hole any-

After practicing your short putts, go back to around 20 feet and try hitting the four balls into the six-foot circle. Keep on knocking them into the circle until you convince yourself it's really quite easy.

thing within three feet, then you don't *have* to get it any closer than three feet on your first putt—and you know you can hole the second putt. Without your trying to, you'll find that one, possibly more, of the four goes right into the hole! The reason is simple. A circle six feet in diameter is a much bigger target than the mere four-and-quarter-inch width of a hole. Practicing aiming for the hole alone will breed tension and miscues. The confidence you get from hitting to the big target will encourage you to swing the putter freely and well.

If you make this procedure a part of your pregame warmup, we can't, of course, promise that you won't ever take three putts again. But at least you should never take more than 36 putts a round, which is an improvement.

There's more controversy about the putting stroke than about any other phase of golf. Of that we are well aware. You'll see more different stances on the putting green than colors in a kaleidoscope. Each has its ardent devotees and each, apparently, enjoys a certain amount of success.

152

For that reason, we are not going to lay down the law on the subject of the address for the putt except to suggest that you play the ball a little more toward the left toe than you would on a chip shot.

On a chip shot you want to catch the ball while the blade is still descending. On the putt it's also important to hit the ball while the blade is still travelling parallel to the ground or even with a slightly closed face, so that the ball will roll truly over the green.

What we think is important is what could be called the problem of the short putt swing.

On the long putts you can still take much the same swing as you take on chip shots. It's like a full swing in miniature. You swing the club, and the body follows the swing. It's a combination of shoulder, arm and hand action with just enough wrist movement to give fluidity to the stroke. (There are two other putting styles. One is full use of the wrists [wrist putting] and shoulder putting [dead hands through the ball].) There may even be a fractional movement in the knees on the back and forward swings, though many good golfers recommend keeping the lower part of the body as still as possible on all putts.

Long-putt stroke. This stroke is much the same as a chip, except the ball is played a little more toward the left toe. Shoulder, arm and hand action combine with enough wrist movement to give a smooth, fluid stroke. Follow through almost as far as you swing back—like the swing of a pendulum. The wider and longer swing arc is necessary to send the ball the required distance.

It's difficult to use the same stroke on the short putts. As you get closer to the hole, you will naturally not swing back as far, that is, the shorter the arc of the swing will become. The shorter the arc, the less

Short-putt stroke. In the tap putt, the club is swung with the hands only, using wrists as hinges. Keep arms and rest of the body still. You literally tap the ball, and the forward action of the clubhead stops a few inches after the ball is struck. Cutting down both the radius and length of swing arc allows you to hit short putts firmly and retain feel of clubhead in your fingers.

speed is generated in the clubhead, and the less centrifugal force there is to keep the club swinging truly.

On the longer putts you can feel the centrifugal force in your fingers, so that you have something definite to tell you that the swing is smooth. But if you use the long putt stroke on these short putts, you will find there is little centrifugal force to feel. This is the reason that so many short putts are wrenched or jerked off line. You get too anxious because you can't feel the clubhead.

It becomes obvious that you should develop a putting stroke that will enable you to hit the short putts without getting a wrench or jerk into the action. One good solution is what is called the "tap" putt.

In the tap putt the stroke is executed with the hands only, using the wrists as hinges. The arms and the rest of the body remain still. This cuts down on the radius of the swing. On the long putt stroke it was from the

154

shoulders to the clubhead. On the tap stroke it is only from the wrists to the clubhead.

In tap putting the forward action of the clubhead stops a few inches after the ball is struck. This cuts down on the arc of the swing, compared with the long putt stroke, which is more like the action of a pendulum with a follow-through similar in length to the backswing.

The two characteristics of the tap putt—the shorter radius of the swing and the shorter swing arc—cut down on the force you get compared with using the same amount of effort with the longer putt stroke. This means you can "tap" your short putts quite firmly and still only send the ball the short distance desired. Better yet, you can again feel the swing of the clubhead in your hands, so that there's no temptation to jerk or wrench the putt off line.

A word of warning. There comes a point where the tap putt will not develop enough force to achieve the required distance and still stay on line. As a rule of thumb, therefore, don't attempt to use the tap stroke on putts of much more than six feet. Forcing the tap stroke is just as senseless as using the long putt stroke for short putts.

Now, if you hole every putt in the six-foot circle and leave all your long putts within the circle—and can do this consistently—then by all means "charge" every putt. Your feel and confidence will be such that even if you miss the cup, you will only be three feet past—and you know you can hole any three-footer. But if you can't go through the whole practice routine without missing a lot of putts, you'll find discretion is the better part of valor.

11. PRO POINTERS ON PUTTING

PUTTING LIKE A PRO

By Billy Casper

When it comes to singling out the most important factor for a low score, putting gets my vote. First, I position myself over the ball and ascertain the direction of the grain and the likely effect it will have on the line my ball must travel to the cup. I place my feet, with my weight distributed evenly, and position my hands on the putter. I use the reverse overlap grip, *employing about the same pressure I would use if I were feeling my pulse.* I bend over just enough to bring my eyes directly over the ball, which I position a bit in front of my left foot and on a line with the inside of my left heel. My feet are about twelve inches apart, with the toe of my left shoe touching the line and my right foot back about an inch from it. I keep my forearms no farther forward than will barely clear my body. I try to hit the ball dead center with the putter, using my wrists almost entirely to power the stroke. I suppose every pro has a favorite bit of putting strategy. Mine is to *concentrate mainly on the distance I need and the amount of speed, not force, I must impart to the ball to get it to the cup firmly enough to clear the near edge and pop in.* And, oh, yes, practice!

LONG PUTT DIVIDENDS

By Fred Hawkins

With 40 feet of green between the ball and the cup, the problems are direction of grain, contour of green and distance. The most important is distance. Three-putting is more often a result of hitting the first putt too hard or too easy than of hitting it off line. On either bent grass or Bermuda greens, the grain, which affects roll, will not usually be uniform throughout; therefore, it should be studied most carefully over the area where the ball is slowing down, that is, around the cup. *The long putt that has break requires a putt of two speeds, one to go over the apex of the break, the other for the remaining distance.* When the ball is stroked hard, the break has little effect; but when the ball begins losing its speed, the contour and grain take over and are factors in the line and distance. Do not make this putt any more difficult than it is by trying to figure the exact break. The green is not a pool table. Instead, *visualize the whole curved path.* About 90 percent of us putt a general line and concentrate on the proper speed. To get the feel of the long putt, I favor the halfway approach, figuring how hard to hit the ball at 20 feet and again at 10 feet from the ball. Note, though, that the 40-foot putt is not stroked twice as hard as the 20-footer. *Once you get the feel, do not return to look again at the line, or else you'll lose everything you've been trying to get.* Then, stand directly over the ball and concentrate on the distance.

GETTING A GRIP ON THE GREENS

By Harold Henning

One of the first things I had to do when I came to the United States from South Africa was to adjust my putting style. The reason was that the greens back home and in other countries of the world in which I have played generally had smoother grass surfaces and I was able to stroke the ball. *Over here I found I had rather to "pop" the ball to keep it on the intended line to the cup. What I did was, in effect, to open my grip— that is, I turned both hands a bit more under the club so that I would see more of the insides of the fingers of my hands. With this grip, as I take the putter back, the left wrist turns under the club and the right hand picks it up a bit. Thus, when I strike the ball, the downward stroke kind of traps the ball and pops it toward the hole.* This keeps the ball going in the direction I want it to go on the somewhat rougher greens on the tour here. Naturally the other basic fundamentals of this phase of the game must be adhered to, regardless of the individual's style. Even among the professionals with whom I've played, on both sides of the ocean, I might add, there is a noticeable variance in methods used. The successful ones, however, keep the body still, the head stationary over the ball, and each takes the putter blade back low to the ground. I hope the changes I made prove to be of benefit to the average American golfer who has trouble keeping the putts on line on the greens he plays.

160

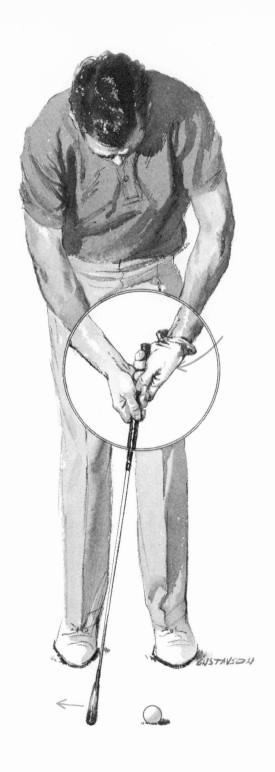

BE A SQUARE ON THE GREEN

By Bob Gardner

You have to be a square if you want to be a good putter—by this I mean have a square stance and keep the putting blade square to the hole. If you also keep your body still, you have a chance to start holing some good putts. When you watch a high handicap player, you will often notice a tendency to cut across the ball. *This can be due to body movement on the downstroke which pushes the ball off to the left or to the fact that the blade is not kept square to the hole.* The high-handicapper has a tendency to scrape the ball. Don't be fearful of hitting with firmness, using a stroke *much as if you were tapping a tack into the wall.* The good player is an aggressive putter who taps the ball firmly. I played recently with a high-handicapper who couldn't sink a putt. I noticed that, as he started his stroke, invariably his right knee moved. After I suggested that he eliminate this movement and keep his body and head still, he suddenly began putting much better. *It is up to the individual as to whether he putts with his wrists or his arms.* Arnold Palmer is a very wristy putter. Gary Player hardly seems to move his hands at all. Billy Casper, regarded as one of the best putters, is a jabber. *But what you'll notice in all of them is that they have a square stance, keep the blade square to the line, keep the blade low, remain still and stroke with authority.*

162

RELEASE THAT PUTTER

By Raymond Floyd

An overlooked phase in putting—I think it is the most important tip on this part of the game—is the release. I don't mean a release that will let you fling the club high over some tree after you've missed a straight one from two feet, going uphill. *The true release in putting refers to a follow-through, similar to the one every golfer is familiar with in executing other shots. It means continuing the stroke through the ball after impact is made.* On tour one sees three types of release: (1) the type used by the "pop" putter, somewhat like that used when you punch an iron shot. (2) The turn of the blade style, by those players who pronate and supinate their wrists when hitting their tee and fairway shots. (3) The stroke style, or the stiff-wristed method. Use whichever way suits you, but make certain you are consistent with it. *The putt will not have a chance if you quit on it.* Releasing the putter works well for me. I am an arm and shoulder putter, hitting through the ball with no wrist break. The palms of my hands are opposite each other and I stroke the shot with the right palm facing the hole. Both hands continue on the line well after the ball leaves the clubface, and *the longer the putt, the longer the release or follow-through. This is just as necessary with a putter as with every other club in your bag, and it must be just as natural. To pay its best dividends, the release with the putter should be the result of a smooth stroke.*

PUTTING FAST GREENS

By Art Wall, Jr.

On extremely fast, slippery greens, putt cautiously and with a lot of thought. A "charged" putt may leave you in a more difficult position than you faced originally. If, however, you do putt boldly on fast greens, allow for less break because the faster the ball is moving the better it will hold the line. And you probably will make quite a few of your short putts this way. On the other hand, though, you are always taking the risk of leaving yourself open to three-putting, even from a very short starting distance. *Course management, conditions of play and the type of competition come into play more than ever on fast greens.* However, in all events, it will be more advantageous to leave yourself with more uphill or straight-in putts, even a few sidehill putts, rather than those dangerous downhill putts. Downhill putts on fast greens can slide away from the hole too easily and put you in a precarious position for three-putting. *The point is, then, to attempt to stop your shots on the putting surface somewhere below or beside the hole, rather than above it.* This is what I mean by good course management and, while it applies to all kinds of greens, it is particularly important on fast greens.

166

PUTTING SLOW GREENS

By Mason Rudolph

When I find myself on slow greens, I make a slight alteration in my putting style. *I "move" the ball a bit forward in my stance, more toward the left toe. At the same time, I move my hands a bit forward, too. The purpose of this is to catch the ball slightly on the upswing on the putt. This gives it more forward motion, which is what you must have to get the ball to the hole on slow greens.* It's not necessary to adjust as much as this when the putt is a downhill one because, of course, the ball naturally rolls faster downhill. When I encounter slow greens, I prefer a putter with a little loft on the face. It sems to give the ball more momentum. One thing you must guard against when putting slow greens is a tendency to "pull" the putt, sending it off line to the left. This can happen because you have to stroke the ball a little more strongly than usual. There is nothing mechanical that can serve as a guard against pulling a putt. You simply must take mental precautions against it.

PUTTING WITH THE GRAIN

By Joe Campbell

A putt with the grain will not break as much as one across or against the grain and it demands a softer, slower roll. For this reason, I recommend two adjustments in the stroking of a putt that is going to roll with the grain. *If you use a blade, a bull's-eye or even a mallet-head putter, you will get a softer roll of the ball by striking it somewhat toward the toe of the face of the club, rather than dead center.* This soft roll is particularly important on fast greens, such as those we play each year at Pebble Beach, for instance. *When your with-the-grain putt is to roll downhill, you can slow up its momentum by stroking the top half of the ball.* There are few putts more fearful than the downhill, slippery putt on fast greens. Getting the ball to behave somewhat better by hitting the top half seems like an unorthodox way to achieve this—and it does call for a lot of skill, practice and know-how, but try both methods. You will soon develop the ability to control the distance the ball rolls. Remember, though, that the slow-moving ball is at the mercy of any unevenness or breaks in the green. One other point to remember: When you are putting along a level or uphill line, you don't have to concern yourself as much with the speed of the ball—except to be sure it's going to reach the hole— because it's not going to run very far past the hole in any event. *Keep in mind that the putt with the grain will not break as much as the others as you line it up.*

PUTTING AGAINST THE GRAIN

By Tommy Jacobs

I consider a putt into the grain one of the most difficult putts a golfer encounters on the green. On a green with a smooth surface and no grain, the ball will roll along a true path until it either goes in or runs out of gas. The exact opposite occurs when a putt is stroked into a thick grain. Most putts are stroked to impart enough speed to carry approximately a foot past the cup—if the ball doesn't drop into the hole. Thus the ball has lost most of its momentum by the time it reaches the hole. The less the speed of the putt, the greater the probability that it will be thrown off line by the grain of the grass. So I suggest two important things to remember when you stroke a putt into the grain. *One is to get the ball rolling with good overspin, which will help it hold the line.* To get this overspin, try to hit up a little bit more than normal on the ball. *The other, of course, is to hit the ball a little harder than usual because the resistance of the grain into which you are putting is bound to slow the ball down more quickly.*

PUTTING ACROSS THE GRAIN

By Paul Harney

It is obvious that the putt traveling across the grain will have a one- to two-inch break in the direction of the grain. What is never so obvious is when such a situation exists. The first order of business, therefore, is to check the green from enough angles to determine whether the green is fast or slow and how pronounced the grain is. *Many times it is difficult to spot the direction of the grain, but if the sun is bright, you'll know that you'll be with the grain if the grass is shiny, against the grain if it is dull.* Putting across the grain means you are at right angles to it, and you must allow for the ball to be affected, most especially around the cup when it begins to slow down. On fast greens this type shot is awfully delicate—as most everyone found out at Oakmont during the '62 Open. I do not suggest or encourage any change in style. No two persons have the same type of stroke, and there is no way of proving that one is more efficient than another. The main concern is to repeat the stroke time after time until a groove has been developed and you are stroking the ball solidly. When this becomes automatic, you will be able to roll the ball over any type of green, directly at the target. *If there is a cross grain, allow for it by playing the ball to break an inch or two accordingly. Change nothing else. And stroke the ball solidly.*

174

PUTTING WET GREENS

By Mike Souchak

Perhaps the most important thing to remember when putting on wet greens is that the ball will not break nearly as much as on dry greens. Because of this, you must be careful not to play as much break on these putts. It goes practically without saying that you must stroke the ball more firmly than on dry greens. This, incidentally, should work to your advantage because, when you can stroke the ball firmly, it will hold the line much better. Actually, when I'm putting wet greens, the hole looks a little bigger to me and this, of course, gives me more confidence on these putts. You should always take two precautions before putting on a wet green. *First, check the line of your putt for particularly damp spots which often develop when it rains.* I don't mean visible water because this constitutes "casual water" and you do not have to putt through casual water. *But some spots on greens will become more damp than others and, if you have to putt over them, they will slow up the ball and your putt will come up short of the hole if you don't allow for it. Second, after you have taken your practice strokes on the green before actually addressing the ball, check the face of your putter to be sure its wet surface has not picked up grass cuttings or other small impediments.* Any such object on the putter face can either deaden the putt and bring it up short or throw the putt off line.

GOLF EXTRA:
THE SCHENECTADY PUTTER

By C. D. Wagoner

Schenectady, N.Y. has probably contributed more to the game of golf than any other city in the United States, not in champions but in equipment that has been universally accepted by golfers all over the world.

Outstanding in the city's contributions have been the Schenectady putter, the first club ever built with the shaft protruding from the center of the head, and the steel shaft club. Both were the inventions of one man, Arthur F. Knight, better known as "Bill" by his friends. Oddly enough, both clubs were designed by Knight, not for commercial profit, but to improve his own game. However, their popularity spread so widely that royalties netted Knight approximately $750,000.

When Knight took up golf about 50 years ago, his greatest handicap was his putting. Being an engineer, then associated with the General Electric Company, he went to work with his slide rule and drawing board hoping he could design a new club that would improve his putting. It took him six years before he perfected a putter that really helped his game. He introduced the club at the Mohawk Golf Club in Schenectady in 1902. It attracted wide attention, some of it unfavorable because of its unorthodox design, but this didn't bother Knight. He was happy that it improved the one weak spot in his game.

Among the enthusiastic endorsers of the new club was Deveroux Emmet, one of Schenectady's best golfers. He took it to Garden City, N. Y., where he knew one of the country's best golfers, Walter J. Travis, would be engaged in tournament play. Travis was shown the putter, he tried it out, liked it in preference to his Scottish type putter, and asked that one be made for him. Using this new type putter, Travis won the United States championship in 1904. He later won the British championship, but his putter so riled the British that this club was officially barred from all future match play in 1910. It was not until 1933 that the ban was lifted.

178

During the 23 years of its prohibition in England, the putter's popularity spread throughout the United States and brought forth an endorsement from William H. Taft, then President of the United States. President Taft sent a letter to Walter J. Travis, telling how much he enjoyed using the Schenectady putter and that it had improved his game. So far as is known, this is the only time a President has lent endorsement to a golf club.

Seven years after he had patented the putter, Knight made his second contribution, the steel shaft club. Again, that invention was brought about by Knight's desire to improve his own game. Seeking to get a greater "whip" to his driver, Knight reduced the diameter of his wooden shaft. But it made his driver unreliable for direction. It was then he began experimenting with steel. He found that the steel shaft produced the desired results and helped to improve his game. This contribution brought him about $250,000 in royalties.

However, he ran into the same trouble as he did with his putter. It was not until the steel shaft had been in use for 12 years that it was legalized in this country. The British were slower to accept the steel shaft and did not lift the ban until 20 years later.

In addition to Knight's major contribution, four other Schenectadians made nationally recognized improvements to the game. The means for providing the perfect balancing of clubs, known as the Swing Weight system, was developed by another General Electric engineer, I. R. Prentice. The Cash-In putter, a streamlined model of the Schenectady putter with a narrower head, was developed by Robert Cash, also a GE engineer. The Limber Shaft club, particularly helpful for beginners in that it helps teach them to wait for the club head to swing through, was jointly developed by Carl F. Mensing and James K. Thompson, the latter golf pro at the Mohawk Golf Club the past 40 years. The latest contribution is bouncing putty, a silicone product of General Electric, widely used for the center or core of golf balls in place of rubber.

VI.   PRACTICE FOR PROFIT

Most golfers are well aware of the importance of practicing, but few know how to go about it in the proper way. You can cut the time you spend at the practice tee and build your game to peak efficiency by applying the suggestions that follow.

12. SWING THE CLUBHEAD

By Nick Martino

The great Bobby Jones said it: "One of the most helpful of all the 'short lessons in golf'—for which I believe Ernest Jones was responsible—is without doubt contained in the maxim, 'Swing the clubhead.' "

I feel fortunate to have spent the majority of my 25 years in golf being associated with Ernest Jones, certainly one of the finest teachers of the game in the world, and I've learned to appreciate the golden truth of that Bobby Jones observation through hundreds of hours on the lesson tee.

"What's wrong with my swing?" If I've heard that once, I've heard it a thousand times. My answer—unless I have a hypochondriacal scratch golfer on my hands—is invariably, "There's nothing wrong with your swing, because *what you're doing isn't a swing at all!*" Yet so badly is the swing misunderstood by the majority of golfers that every awkward, lurching, heaving, swaying action made, alas, by far too many weekend golfers is still called "my swing."

To most golfers struggling to break 100, the swing is a hodgepodge of half-understood—and mostly negative—catch phrases that they must perform one after the other in a time span of less than two seconds. "Don't bend the wrist until the club is waist high, don't bend the left arm, don't fly the right elbow, turn the shoulders, turn the hips but only half as much. . . ." Need I go on? The horrible result of all this is what my good friend Ernest Jones would call "Paralysis By Analysis." Most of these maxims are the *results,* not the causes, of a good swing.

What is a swing? According to Webster, a swing means to move to and fro, back and forth, like a pendulum. It has a definite form, which is part of a circle or an arc. The longer the arc, the greater the speed, and the greater the force of return. A swing, therefore, is one, continuous, indivisible, free-flowing motion; not a succession of small movements. You would never think of drawing a circle freehand by making one short

182

stroke after another. You would draw it in one, bold motion. You should do the same in golf.

Why, you may ask, should one swing at all? The reason is quite simple; a swinging motion produces centrifugal force, the greatest force your body can generate. And the better you learn to swing, the greater force you will develop.

Dramatic demonstration of the power of centrifugal force. Both the "hammer" and the "shot" are 16 pounds, yet a good hammer thrower can send the weight over 200 feet while the shot putter can throw only a little over 60 feet.

One of the most dramatic demonstrations of the power of centrifugal force that comes to mind in an Olympic year is the hammer throw compared with the shot put. Both the "hammer" and the "shot" are 16 pounds in weight, yet a good hammer thrower can send the weight over 200 feet while an athlete putting the shot is doing well to better 60 feet. The hammer thrower uses the power of centrifugal force, while the shot putter relies on a strong push.

Why swing the clubhead? In golf you can only use the clubhead to strike the ball, and most of the weight of the club is in the clubhead. Force is speed squared times weight; therefore, it's logical to swing the weight, or clubhead, at the ball with speed in order to get the greatest centrifugal force.

Now you acquire a golf swing through a sense of "feel," a sensation of having control of the swinging motion of the clubhead at all times during the swing. You may have heard of "acquiring clubhead feel," "getting the feel of the swing" and similar expressions. Here's what they mean.

183

You hold the club in your hands. They are the only part of the entire body making direct contact with the club, and are therefore the only possible medium through which the power in your body can be transmitted to the club. It follows that you feel the swinging clubhead in your hands and fingers alone. We can even be more precise.

When you lift a cup of coffee, which fingers do you use? I think you will find you use the thumb and forefinger. One or two of the other fingers may act as helpers, but the thumb and forefinger do the real work.

Now lift the cup with your other hand. The result will be the same.

So the thumb and forefinger of each hand are the principal fingers and it is in them, primarily, that you should *feel* the swinging clubhead. As with the coffee cup, the other fingers act as helpers. (In golf, of course, we hold the club with both hands so they should hold the club as though they were one unit.)

Maybe you noticed another thing as you brought the coffee to your lips. Your arm, and possibly your shoulder, also moved. However, the arm and shoulder followed the lead of the thumb and forefinger; they didn't initiate the action.

It should be the same in golf. Because we have larger muscles in other parts of our bodies such as the arms and shoulders, these parts tend to want to get going too soon. But they must be regarded as admirable followers of the hands, but disastrous as leaders. You swing the clubhead with your hands, and the rest of your body should follow its lead.

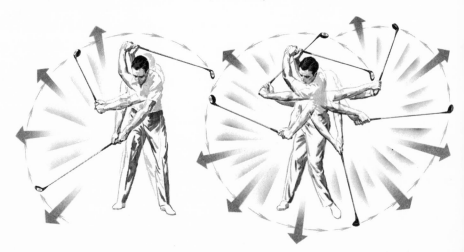

At all times during the swing, you will feel in your hands a constant pull by the clubhead caused by the centrifugal force you are generating.

184

You will find that if you swing the clubhead with your hands *from the start to the finish of the swing,* you will feel a constant pull by the clubhead in the hands at all times. This outward pull—cause by the centrifugal force being generated gradually and smoothly in the clubhead—will make you swing back in a wide arc, keep your left arm extended, shift your weight and all the other myriad things you have been told to do, *automatically.* It keeps your swing in the "groove" because the swing *is* the "groove."

The pull of the swinging clubhead is the reason for the so-caled "late hit." The outward force will hinge the wrists quite naturally on the way back, will at first leave them behind on the downswing, then, as the cen-

Incorrect. The players' hands are not controlling the clubhead. This leads to swaying.

trifugal force builds up, will bring them back square to the ball at impact. It's like the opening of the door which causes its hinges to bend.

Swinging the clubhead will also take care of your balance throughout the swing. Centrifugal force recedes from a center. In the golf swing, the centrifugal force you generate will, through the hands, find its own center or zero point, somewhere in your body. This is the condition of perfect balance in motion. But you don't need to know where the zero point is. It's sufficient that it is there because you are swinging. You can't swing with zero, so you have to swing with your hands.

It is vital, however, for you to swing the clubhead and not to *let it swing. Make it swing so that it swings you.* If you control the swing of the clubhead with your hands at all times, then that zero point somewhere in your body will remain in the same place throughout the swing. Your swing will have a constant center to move around. If you don't allow the

185

clubhead to swing you, then your zero point will shift around all over the place and no sort of consistency can result.

Unfortunately for themselves, golfers will—either from fear or tension —stiffen their muscles at some time during the swing, and often even at address. Or they exert leverage by allowing the big muscles of the arms or shoulders to dominate the action. Worst of all, they rush the golf stroke to such an extent that they *move the club faster than they can swing it,* so that it's no longer, if it ever was, a swing. Any of these faults will destroy a swing or prevent it happening.

To demonstrate this, take hold of a club at the end of the grip with

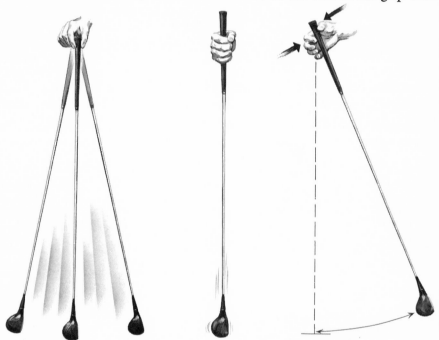

Swing clubhead back and forth like a pendulum, left, and you will feel the weight of swinging club in your thumb and forefinger. Violently grab the handle, center, and the swing stops. Exert leverage, right, and clubhead hardly moves.

your thumb and forefinger and start it swinging back and forth like a pendulum. As you swing it, you will feel the weight of the swinging club in your thumb and forefinger. That's the centrifugal force you're feeling. Notice, too, that to keep it swinging, your hand has to move also a short way in the direction the clubhead is traveling. This proves that, while you are swinging the clubhead with your hand, the hand is not the zero point, but that this is somewhere in your body.

186

Now grab the club violently with the rest of your hand. What happened? Your arm went stiff as a ramrod from the shoulder down—and the clubhead *stopped swinging*. This is what tension can do to the swing.

Again start swinging the clubhead as before and get the feel of the swing in your finger and thumb. Now, stop the clubhead with your other hand, and then try to move the clubhead by exerting leverage with the forefinger and the thumb. You will find the clubhead can be moved in a circular arc with such an action, but notice how inferior leverage is as a force to move the clubhead compared to the swing. You will be lucky to move it two inches away from the vertical. It's the hammer throw and shot put all over again.

Another excellent way to get the feel of the swing is with a device I'll now describe. It consists of a three-foot piece of shock cord, at one end of which is attached a sponge-like ball, about three inches in diameter. It's commercially available, but you can make one yourself.

Wrap the end of the cord a few turns around your left hand and then bring your right hand onto the cord in your regular golf grip. Now start

Starting the swing with the swinging device.

the device swinging, back and forth, like a pendulum, until the rubber shock cord stretches and you have increased the length of the swing arc to a full golf swing.

It may take you a while to learn how to swing this device. But if you do, you will be well on the way toward low-handicap golf. The reason for this is that the flexible shock cord will reveal inexorably any tense or jerky actions or leverage you exert. As you swing it back and forth, you will find you can gradually extend the arc as centrifugal force stretches the cord. You can also swing the device and a regular club together to test whether you are swinging or not.

A lot of people *think* they swing a golf club. But when they try to swing this device, they realize they are using jerky motions, of one sort or another, and end up with the ball wrapped around their necks—if it ever gets back that far!

If you swing it correctly, the centrifugal force you're generating in the swinging ball will cause the cord to stretch and it will remain taut as you swing it back. At the top of the swing it will wrap around your back a little, but if you keep swinging, it will go through with a tremendous "swoosh" of centrifugal force—*this is the feel you get when you swing a golf club*. Incidentally, this is how a trick-shot artist like Paul Hahn can swing a golf club with a flexible or jointed shaft.

Now the swing is the same from the drive to the putt. You just swing the clubhead with your hands. However, just as the spinning top will keep perfectly in its groove when it is spinning at its maximum and falls over when the spin is exhausted, so even fine golfers find more difficulty with the short game than the long. The smaller the arc, the less clubhead speed is generated—and the more likely it is that you will use leverage to get results because there is less outward pull of centrifugal force to keep your swing going. But it *is* possible to swing every club in the bag and that's the goal you should aim for.

Constant practice of the golf swing is what enables the touring pro to hit the ball so far. He can swing much harder than you can. But every golfer should find out how hard he can swing without introducing into the swing any of the improper motions discussed above.

Start out by using the seven-iron and playing approach shots. Discard the feeling of having to hit hard, so as to build up rhythm and timing. Your muscles will work in harmony with the swing and you will find you can gradually increase the over-all speed of your swing by enlarging its arc, thus hitting the ball as far as your ability will allow. But you must always keep your speed of swing safely below that point where you run the risk of using leverage, or getting tension. This speed is a personal thing. But you can—and should—use all the speed you can safely handle so you can get maximum force into your swings.

This golf swing won't just happen overnight. It takes practice in golf, as in any other art, to make perfect. But if you swing the clubhead, it will follow the path of least resistance or the proper arc for you, and the whole body will perform as it should. Don't worry if other golfers say to you, "Your swing is too upright, too flat, too this or that." Just smile smugly to yourself and keep on swinging!

Forget about the thousand and one bits, or so-called golf secrets. Jack Nicklaus and Arnold Palmer, two of our leading golfers, certainly would be the ones who have the secret if one existed; but are they winning *all the time? No.* Well, then, this proves that there are no secrets or "instant" cures.

When you are not moving the club in a swinging motion—and we are all human, not swinging, machines—you should believe that the swing does exist, being a definite thing, and strive to acquire the feel that only a swinging motion can produce. Remember, swing it, don't *let* it swing. This takes practice, practice and still more practice. But never forget, there's nothing right about wrong. Do what's right and swing the clubhead. Only then will your scoring come nearer to that of the professional golfer.

13. PRO POINTERS ON PRACTICE

HOW TO PRACTICE THE SHORT IRONS

By Jerry Barber

My practice sessions start with the short irons because they enable me to loosen up my muscles and get ready to hit the ball hard. After all, golf is a power game: you really have to hit the ball as hard as you can to play your best. However, it is also a game where finesse around the greens can pay off, too, and to keep this important phase under control, I follow a set routine on the practice tee. *Using a ten-iron (pitching wedge) first, I hit little pitch shots of 25 to 30 yards, pushing the caddie back until I reach the maximum distance of about 85 yards.* This is about the length of a three-quarter nine-iron, which I then work to about 115 or 120 yards. With the eight, I start by hitting shots about the same length as the full nine and move the caddie back to the eight-iron's maximum of about 125 or 130 yards. *Using the same pattern with the seven, I move my caddie out to 135 or 140 yards. From this point, I practice half- and three-quarter shots,* anticipating playing shots into the wind and those which I will want to hit in front of the green and run on. *This phase is especially valuable because it gives a good over-all feel of the clubs from all distances.*

190

MUSCLE MEMORY

By Paul Hahn

Do you think of a thousand things when standing up to hit the ball? Don't. *The best way to use your mind is not to use it while in the swing.* This sounds like some of the double talk I throw into my trick-shot repertoire, but what it means is that *you must develop your stroke to the point where you don't have to think of the component parts when you do swing.* Just concentrate on hitting the ball and everything else will fall into place. *You can actually hit the ball subconsciously if you have muscle memory, if you acquire a muscular groove, a sense of feel.* In developing some two dozen trick shots, I discovered that the sense of feel holds true for every shot in golf. What applies to me is pertinent for the many different shots you must make with the 14 clubs in your bag. Do it with muscle memory, and *get this sense of feel through repetition, by hitting as many shots as you can, staying in the same groove until you can swing subconsciously at the ball, confident that you can depend on your swing.* Confidence in the swing, or muscle memory, gives you the composure which is a trait of every champion.

HOW TO PRACTICE THE MIDDLE IRONS

By Johnny Pott

Practicing with the middle irons can be the real key to getting your timing down with all your clubs. You can get the feel of solid comfort with them because they are of medium length and loft and, by playing the ball in the middle of the stance, they are easier and less awkward to hit. While the average player might be a little scared to hit the driver, he normally isn't afraid of the middle irons. *The most important part of hitting these clubs is the stance, since good balance is necessary for the accuracy we want to get from them during play*. It is essential that balance be worked on during practice. Take a square stance and let the club rest behind the ball just as it is made, with the entire sole almost level to the ground. The swing is to be a full one, but remember to let the club do the work. *Plan to hit down on the ball, hit it first, take turf afterward*. Most of us have found that when we're hitting the middle irons well, we're hitting all the clubs correctly, having then only to change stance and position of the ball.

STRENGTHEN THE LEFT SIDE

By Lyle Wehrman

The game of golf is primarily a left-handed game for a right-handed person, but have you recently tried to grip and swing the club with the left hand only? More often than not the club will waver considerably on the backswing and very few persons will reach the top keeping the club-head in the same plane. Most of us who are natural right-handers will be very strong on the right side, which is the wrong side for the good golf swing. *The controlling factors in the swing are the left hand and arm.* To reach the point where you will begin to hit the ball better, you must strengthen them. *Any exercise such as squeezing a sponge ball or any foam rubber or plastic aid that will resist this motion of the hand and fingers is good, but I recommend that you spend as much time as possible actually swinging the club with the left arm only.* You will strengthen those important muscles and get them accustomed or attuned to the job they must do. When you have reached the point where you can make the backswing with the left hand almost as smoothly as you can with both, not only will you find that you have increased your distance on all your shots, but your accuracy will improve as well.

196

SLOW SWING CAN END SLUMPS

By Billy Milward

All of us—professionals and weekend golfers alike—can go into a slump. However, where the professionals and weekenders diverge is the way they go about getting out of the slump. *Most golfers merely compound their troubles by trying to hit harder. This makes just about as much sense as driving across a bridge that is about to be swept away by a flood.* You would never think of overloading a bridge in that condition, so why impose further strain on a creaky swing? Next time you lose your timing, go out to the practice tee and set about it this way. *Take a short iron and consciously draw the club back slower than you normally do. Swing back a little shorter than usual and meticulously time the hit, concentrating all your attention on making solid contact with the ball.* Once you start hitting it on the nose, you can take a full short-iron swing, but still keep the tempo of the swing rather slower than usual. Then move up through your middle and long irons to your woods. Remember, swing slower than normal. *You are trying to build up your timing, not hit the ball a ton.* However, I think you will be surprised how far you can hit with this slow swing—I can get 200 to 220 yards with my driver. Once your timing is re-established, then by all means increase the tempo until you have reached the speed of swing that is best for you.

DEVELOPING RHYTHM

By Vincent Grillo

This simple exercise will help you develop rhythm, shift your weight automatically and give correctness to your body turn without thinking. *Place your hands on the club about 24 inches apart, palms facing down, a few inches from your body, in a position to freely initiate the backswing.* Take your normal address position, but look at some object on the floor that is in the center of your stance. *Start the club back as though actually swinging, taking the hands above the shoulder,* getting the shaft horizontal—or as nearly so as possible—to the floor. Do not take your eyes off the object. *The feeling should be in your hands, not in the arms, since that is where the control of the swing should be.* Now start the downswing. *The weight of the club and the momentum of the exercise will carry you through the full swing.* If you find that you do not get the feeling in the hands, something is interfering with the motion. Free yourself of tension and start again.

PRACTICE WHAT IS PREACHED

By Andy Gibson

Taking golf lessons is like taking piano lessons: what good are they if you don't do any subsequent practicing? Too many persons expect a miracle from a meeting with their professional instructor, apparently thinking that the mere taking of one lesson should make them score better the next time they play. This is an impossibility unless they rehearse what they were taught and have made the lesson session a part of their game. *The biggest drawback to rushing out to play too soon after a lesson is that you end up devoting the entire round to thinking about what the pro has taught and you miss the true benefits of the round of golf.* Instead of showing improvement, your game retrogresses. I find that *a good formula is to practice about one hour for every half-hour lesson you take, broken up so that you devote no more than 30 minutes at any one time on the practice tee* absorbing what was taught. Two half-hour sessions over two days following each lesson will set you up perfectly for more enjoyable golf. Only on the practice tee can you find the atmosphere to think about the points covered and the time to make them routine.

THE PRACTICE AREA

By Marlene Bauer Hagge

All top men and women golfers consider the practice tee their workshop. To them it is more than just a place to visit and get the feel of the clubs and/or loosen up the golfing muscles. Rather, it is the place that the stars hone their games to the high levels needed for tournament play. There are no rules or even agreements on just how long one should practice. I feel I can get some good out of these sessions as long as I can maintain concentration. Once I feel that I'm just stepping up and hitting the ball without plan, I know it's time to quit. *In starting a normal practice stint, I always pick out a short iron first, since it requires the least effort to use. I believe that timing and coordination should be gained—or regained— gradually. After I've worked up to some drives, I always conclude with a few short pitch shots.* The practice tee is also the place to solve any problem, and even several hours spent on it would not be wasted as long as concentration is maintained. And this brings up the final hint: *Do not practice when you are tired.* Many golfers rush out after a round of golf to iron out some difficulty, unaware or unmindful that they may be physically, if not also mentally, exhausted. *This can have discouraging results, because when you are tired, your timing is affected, and if this occurs, nothing will help.* It is then best to sit down and think it over, map out your strategy and work out on the tee the next day.

HOW TO PRACTICE PUTTING

By Bob Rosburg

You practice putting to improve your touch or to get the feel of the greens. *Therefore, take only three or four balls with you,* not the whole bag, *and try putts of varying lengths.* Try a couple of 20-footers, a few 40-footers, then some short ones. If you putt a whole bag of balls from the same distance, you'll develop a stereotyped stroke. You'll be just going through the motions without having to think about what you're doing. *If you are working on perfecting your stroke and getting something that feels comfortable, take the easiest type of putt you can have, a four- or five-footer straight uphill.* If you practice those, your stroke will come back and you'll get more confidence. Then you can work on those tricky downhill and sidehill putts. *Another tip is to practice putting to a spot that is smaller than the regulation hole,* perhaps at a water sprinkler on the green. When you get to hitting that spot every time, the regular hole will seem bigger to you out on the course. Some practice greens have these half-sized holes, and I think it's a great idea. As for styles of putting, I feel it's mainly finding a stance and a grip that are comfortable and effective. There are successful putters with all kinds of individual differences. *But about the stroke, never allow the right hand to pass the left, and make certain you have the clubhead accelerating when it hits the ball.* I don't think anyone has the nerves to putt successfully with the clubhead losing speed when it strikes the ball: you can't always keep the clubface square that way, and the stroke becomes inconsistent. *When you do hit the ball squarely every time, you've got putting at least 50 percent beat.*

PRACTICE ACQUIRING CLUBHEAD FEEL

By Art Vogt

Golf efficiency depends in a great measure on "feel" and therefore can change according to how well tuned you are to the job at hand. This means that *there is a definite, tangible link between the way the club feels to your hands and the way you hit the ball.* I advocate the swinging hit which calls for accelerated pressure because the greatest speed has to be at the lowest point of the swing *according to your feeling.* But this low point changes as your "touch" varies, sometimes from day to day. The actual snap into the ball might start eight inches from the ball one time, 12 inches behind another time, or right at the ball on other occasions. *This sensation can be checked out in practice: Grip the club as you would normally and just let it hang. The weight of the club itself will keep the arms extended as much as they should be extended.* No need to make the common error of locking the shoulders in an attempt to keep the left arm stiff. Now they are relaxed, *straight without stiffness. Put a golf ball in the palm of each hand and hold onto the club with only the thumb and forefinger of both hands.* You will really feel the drag of the club as it hangs because it will seem to weigh a ton. You won't be able to squeeze the butt end, you can't fight it, in fact you can hardly hold it. But *take a swing at a ball.* The club will not slip up into the fleshy part of the right hand, and *you should discover that you'll actually be able to hit the ball about 160 yards—proving that efficient acceleration of the clubhead does more to produce distance than brute force, poorly timed. This is the swinging hit.*

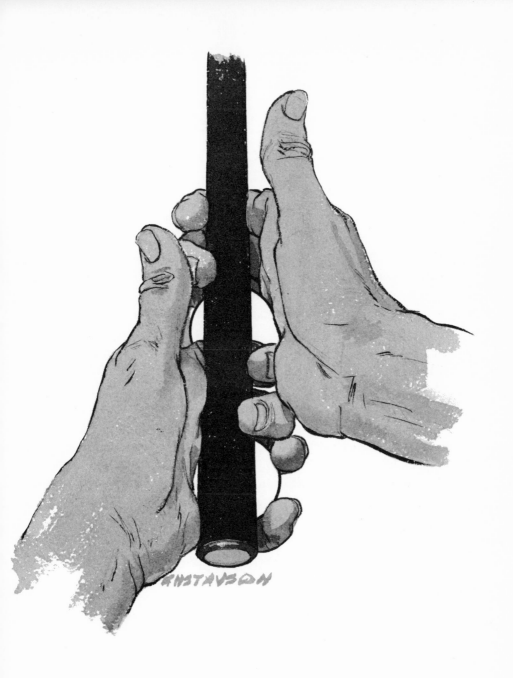

HOW TO PRACTICE CHIPPING

By Gardner Dickinson, Jr.

Chipping deserves at least 15 minutes of daily practice for an accomplished player, longer for others. *Vital to success are two facts: keep the clubface square to the line of flight at contact, and keep most of the weight on the left side from a slightly open stance.* I am a wrist chipper. I prefer this style because it limits the number of clubs I have to learn for my chipping, and I know the effective distances for each of them. Basically, *wrist-chipping means keeping the top or grip end of the club in the same position,* perhaps even moving slightly toward the hole. I also break my wrists slightly under, which takes some of the loft off the club. Then I try to do only one thing—return to my original starting position. This means that, with the short distance backswing and the wrists broken to a maximum, the clubhead action has to be very rapid. *I never break my right hand under my left as I go through the ball* and so get a lower flight, which I think is desirable, while getting the ball over the fringe, which can result in unpredictable bounces. My practice sequence usually starts with the wedge and ends with the seven-iron. I seldom go lower, but on occasions have used the six when I couldn't avoid landing on the fringe. The objective in chipping is to land the ball on the green and start it rolling. Very few players will chip with intentional backspin on the ball.

PLANNED PRACTICE PAYS OFF

By Al Maus

I don't know why it is so, but a golfer is usually a man who sits in an office all week, and then thinks he can come right out on the first tee and whack a 300-yard drive down the middle. Whether or not this describes you, *always try to hit a few practice shots before starting out.* If practice doesn't make perfect, *at least it will loosen up your muscles. If you are a beginner, I advise your doing all your prepping with the driver.* This is the hardest club to master, of course, but it will help set a swing tempo that can be carried into actual play with all clubs. *A three-quarter swing with the No. 1 wood helps control this shot and will make the rest of the clubs easier to manipulate. The low-handicapper should begin from the other end, starting with the high-trajectory irons and working up through the long irons and then to the woods.* In either case, be intelligent about this chore: You can hit more of a variety of shots from the practice tee in 30 minutes than you can in a four- or five-hour round. If you are about to play, do not overdo it. *Be satisfied to develop rhythm.* If you have completed your round, practice to rid yourself of those shots that caused you trouble. *The practice area will pay off big dividends when you have and follow a preconceived plan.*

212

GOLF EXTRA:
HOW TO TAKE A LESSON

By Peggy Kirk Bell

Much has been written about the art of *teaching* golf. However, the importance of the art of *taking* a lesson has been generally overlooked. While it does not require any physical skill, you must use a modicum of common sense.

First and foremost, be honest with your golf professional and tell him exactly what you are trying to accomplish. Do you want a complete picture of the golf swing or do you just want to play for the exercise? Are you willing to practice or don't you have the time? Is this lesson to be one of a series or a one-shot deal?

Having your objectives clear at the start and making them known to the instructor can save both of you a lot of grief.

Being honest with the pro doesn't stop there. Reveal any physical handicaps you may have—however minor—that could affect the way you swing. To cite an extreme case, I once worked a solid hour with a pupil trying to get him to transfer his weight to the left leg on the downswing. At the end of the hour, he confided to me that this would be difficult for him since he had an artificial leg!

Another problem I have with many of my pupils is that they are not good listeners. Their one idea is to belt as many balls as they can in the allotted time. Remember, it's impossible to get your money's worth if you insist on hitting while the instructor is explaining something. Only by listening will you be able to absorb it.

There is, also, the golfer who comes onto the lesson tee with just a driver and says, "I slice everything." I take a look at his swing—and the slices—and reply, "Well, if we could take your five-iron and get the swing going on the inside, then I think we can lick this." By now he's so mad he says, "If I can't hit the driver, I just won't play golf." There are none so deaf as those who will not hear!

Listening to your golf professional entails carrying out what he's telling you—even if it doesn't feel comfortable for a time. When you do anything new, it's bound to feel strange at first. It means listening to him, *not* listening to well-meaning, but mostly uninformed advice from your golf buddies.

Be patient about learning the fundamentals. Here, I get the upper body into good position with square clubface.

The right knee should be flexed at the top of the backswing.

Most times friends will say something like, "You're swaying." They may have spotted your fault, but they haven't told you *what to do positively to get you swinging again.* That's the job of teaching the golf swing, and it is your pro's business. Of course, if you prefer a medicine man to a qualified doctor. . . .

A good listener also has patience. Don't expect miracles in five minutes or worry unduly just because you can't hit each shot perfectly. Don't be impatient when your pro tells you he liked the swing, even when you missed! What he means is that you are that much nearer to really swinging the club. So keep at it and, with hard work and patience, you'll be surprised how good you can become.

By patient I *don't* mean standing there like a lemon not understanding a word the pro is saying! Every golf instructor has a golf language. He'll say, "Open your stance," for example, and take for granted that the pupil understands what he is saying. Often the pupil doesn't!

Never be afraid to ask your pro a question. After all, that's what he is there for. This applies to any point he is making, not just golf language. If he knows you don't understand, he can usually find another way of putting it which will be clear to you.

Learning special shots pays off. When playing off a bare lie, to a hard green with no traps in between, discard your wedge, use a straighter-faced club, play the ball nearer your right foot and run it.

Here's an example of how a playing lesson can help you. By choosing the right tee-off spot, you can play straight at the pin without having to play over the trap on the left.

Many people are too anxious when they go for a lesson. They tighten up and can hardly hit a shot. Many women come to me saying, "Oh, I've never played any sport and I just know I'm going to be terrible." They apologize for taking the lesson even before they start! This sort of attitude will get you "nowhere fast!"

Remember, fear and the golf swing don't mix. Confidence, on the other hand, is one of the best tonics for a golf swing I know.

Now, even if you have a reasonably good swing, don't imagine your lesson days are over. There is much more to golf than just learning to swing a club, though I'll admit that most golfers don't ever get that far.

216

Do you have problems with that troublesome little pitch over a trap? Do you know how to play the ball to run? Can you get out of a trap? There are all sorts of shots where you must adapt the basic swing to different circumstances. Your pro is the person who can help you learn these finer points.

It is also a fact that even if pupils have all the shots, I often find they don't know where to use them on a golf course. Or they just don't line themselves up to hit the ball in the right direction. The best place to learn how to play a course is *on* the course during a playing lesson.

It's really a shame that the golfers who could benefit most by seeing how a good golfer uses his head during a round usually play with golfers who are not much better than they are. So they *never* learn to play a course. I think that my pupils have learned more during a playing lesson than if they had stood on a practice tee for ten hours!

So next time you take a lesson:
1. Be honest with your pro and state your objectives.
2. Listen to him—and only him—and do what he tells you.
3. Be patient—the golf swing, like Rome, is not built in a day.
4. Be confident—remember, fear will make a paralyzed rabbit out of anyone!
5. Ask your pro questions—he won't bite!

VII. TROUBLESOME SHOTS AND SITUATIONS

It is virtually impossible for even the finest golfer to completely avoid trouble in any round of golf. The big difference however, between the weekend player and the pro is the way they go about getting out. The pro refuses to panic and instead spends his time figuring the best possible shot he can *reasonably* expect to make. Learn here how you too, can recover from trouble with the minimum loss of strokes.

14. THE ART OF SCRAMBLING

By Doug Ford

As long as the emphasis is on power golf, any player who hopes to reach the top must be a super "scrambler," and if this is true for the tournament performer (which it is), it would have to go double for the rest of the golfing fraternity.

This is an era in which longer golf courses are being built, and these new layouts usually don't have the heavy growth of the established shorter courses. Consequently, everybody is either banging the ball in a quest for birdies or going all out just trying to keep up with par on these king-sized holes. But when you unload all your power, you sacrifice accuracy. Once you stray from the straight and narrow, you have to start scrambling.

The scrambler, be he professional or amateur, has the special talent to be able to get the ball into position for that saving one-putt. This requires great proficiency with the scoring clubs, from the five through the sand iron, so that you can chip and run, lob your pitch or play a running shot as the case requires. I have said that the average player should be as good a scrambler as the better player for the obvious reason that he *has* to scramble more often. Therefore, it seems to me that this person should practice a lot more with the scoring clubs so that he knows without question how each one reacts every time.

Most high-handicap players use a "favorite" club on all their short pitches. This contributes to their high scoring because one club is not fitted for the continually changing circumstances.

For example, there are many factors which must be taken into consideration when you make your pitch shot, the keystone shot for the good scrambler. You must check on the contour of the green to figure out the roll, note whether the grain is with you or against you, and the distance. Reading the green is one of the greatest talents the man who needs those one-putt approaches can have.

220

You might find it to your advantage on an exceptionally long chip to select a five-iron if you are going against the grain and an eight or nine *from the same distance* when going downhill or with the grain or both. You must practice these saving shots, not only to understand them, but to determine how far each club is going to run for you. But, as a general rule of thumb, with the straight-faced clubs such as the five- or six-iron, pitch one-third of the way to the pin and figure on the ball rolling the

Chipping with a straight-faced club, hit the ball one-third of the way to the pin and figure on the ball rolling the remaining distance. Pick out a spot on the green where you want the ball to land and concentrate on hitting there. To eliminate any chance of a bad bounce, always land the ball on the green.

other two-thirds. With the seven or eight, pitch about halfway. With the nine-iron or wedge, cover two-thirds of the way in flight and get one-third run. For a quick stop, get to know how to pitch with the sand wedge from varying distances.

In each instance, pick out a spot on the green where you want the ball to land and concentrate on hitting that spot. If judgment of contour and grain are correct, and you are using the right club to do the job, you should be up there for a saving one-putt green. Another factor to consider is that your shot should land *on* the green. Hitting on the putting surface gives you a truer bounce. If you hit short, you are taking the risk of the ball finding a depression or hole or bump and ruining your shot.

So the actual key, it seems to me, is practicing hitting to a certain spot and observing the distance of the roll you get with each of the scoring clubs. Notice I said clubs. Many foreign players chip with one club, changing the loft by the mechanics of their swing. It is my view that they are making the game a lot harder and, under pressure, might revert to the wrong swing. I don't believe in altering the swing. Let the right club do the work and you have this big battle half won.

The second important axiom in the art of scrambling is not to get upset. Everyone hits bad shots and you must expect to do likewise, at least once in a while. But getting so mad that you can execute neither the subsequent shot nor the succeeding ones properly will do you no good.

Poor planning usually seems to be the biggest cause of golfers getting into trouble, and this can take place *anywhere* on the course. For example, even the first tee shot can be a scramble for a majority of players because, before starting a round in a tournament, there almost always is a feeling of tightness. Usually this leaves you after the first shot, but you can be real nervous when you're nursing a slim lead or have a chance to win during the final round.

By planning I mean selecting an area to hit to that will cost you the least penalty if something goes wrong. I try to anticipate my errors under pressure and plan to face the lesser of two evils if I do miss.

But sometimes even the best plans backfire. I recall an instance where on two consecutive holes I scrambled my way out of real trouble and had I started blowing my stack, I don't know what might have happened.

This was during the 1962 Bing Crosby National at Pebble Beach. Going into the last hole, a 400-yarder, I was one shot behind Joe Campbell and my playing partner Ken Venturi didn't really have to tell me I needed a birdie to tie. The pin was tucked back into the left corner of the green, and my initial plan was to play my tee shot to favor the right

To fade, open your stance, play the ball forward and draw the club back on the outside.

To hook, the ball is played farther back. The closed stance should cause an inside-out swing.

side of the fairway. It went dead center, but long enough to leave me an eight-iron shot to the stick. Being familiar with the contour of the green, I decided to hook the approach shot with this club so that the ball would kick in toward the pin. To hook or fade, I change my stance to closed or open, respectively, and I do the same with the clubface, swinging inside out (and flatter) for a hook, outside in (and upright) for the fade. But the grip remains the same.

Thinking I had covered all angles, I hit the hook I wanted. But what I didn't remember was that the grain ran in the same direction as the shot I was playing. The result was the ball kicked too much and ran across the green and down into the rough area near some trees.

Luck was with me, however, and when I got to the ball, I found that I not only had a fine lie, but the ball had come to rest about 15 feet to the left of the green and another 15 feet to the pin, an ideal distance to approach with a pitch and run shot. Without hesitation—a very helpful

223

idea, at times—I selected a wedge, lofted the ball about three-quarters of the way onto the green and *it rolled in—for a tie!* This stroke (of luck) put me in a sudden-death playoff but I almost immediately found myself in trouble again, this time with sand.

Now, any good recovery player is one who is also a fine trap player. Once you have this shot under control, once it becomes almost second nature, you're in business because you'll find times when you would prefer being in a bunker rather than facing a tremendously long putt. I would rather be 15 feet from the pin and in sand any time than try to figure out a 60-foot putt.

And this turned out to be the situation at the first sudden-death hole at the Bing Crosby. The wind was dead against us but we both drove into the heart of the fairway. The pin, this time, was tucked back into the right-hand corner of the green, and to get close I played a left-to-right fade by opening the face of the club and hitting outside in. The ball hit on the green all right but then rolled into a bunker! However, I was pin high and only about 25 feet away.

Joe's second shot just made the green, and he left himself one of those 60 footers I was referring to. He knocked his first putt five feet past the hole. I had yet to hit out of the bunker.

Sand changes in texture and compactness as we play on courses in different locations, but the strategy of this shot remains pretty much the same. I generally hit one and a half inches behind the ball every time, swinging harder if I have to make the ball go farther. The blade is open a bit and the flange on the club is able to do what it is designed to do —ride through the sand. The swing must be smooth and uninterrupted.

Setting myself firmly in the sand, checking one more time the direction of both the grain of the green and the direction of the wind, I exploded out of the trap, the ball stopping inside of Joe's! He missed his putt, I holed mine, and the Bing Crosby tournament was all over.

The toughest of all sand shots is probably the plugged or buried ball, but the problem is usually more fancied than factual. Since you only have to solve this once to realize that this is so, I suggest enough practice *if only to prove it to yourself.* The difference here from a normal trap shot would be to hood (close) the face of the wedge. Then the flange in back is *higher* than the club's leading edge so it does *not* do *what it is designed* to do and bounce off the sand into the ball. You might even try using a nine-iron.

224

When the ball is buried, you have to get under it to get it out. This calls for a little more power in the swing than for an average trap shot because the sand will dissipate the force of the clubhead. Dig in firmly, anticipate

The majority of golfers open the clubface when playing a trap shot. This would be correct if the lie were good. But in these photos the ball is partially buried. Golfer shown at the left has moved up properly but has retained the open clubface. This is the wrong combination. To solve this problem, square the clubface so that the bottom line is at a right angle to your intended direction and hit about one and one-half inches behind the ball. The shot will pop out and roll.

a lot of run and a hook spin to the ball and swing on through. The ball will almost always pop right out and once in a while will go in.

The year I won the Masters, my approach shot to the seventy-second buried itself in the face of a bunker to the left of the green. You may recall having seen this on TV. The contour of the green called for playing the ball up high so it would run down toward the hole placed in a flat area near the front of the green. I hit down behind the ball with the blade hooded a bit, the ball jumped out onto the green, and it ran down and into the cup!

When you are scrambling—and I've never known a winning player who didn't have to do it, and do it well, and that takes in all of them from Sam Snead to Arnold Palmer—you also have to have a little bit of luck going for you. Like that trap shot at Augusta National, or that almost perfect lie even though I was in the woods on the final hole where I caught Campbell.

I remember another instance, vividly, even though it happened in 1953. Playing in the Miami Open that year, I was 30 yards short of the green on the long, par-five fifteenth hole. The green was contoured from left to right and I was just trying to get close. I planned a regular pitch shot with very little run, knowing that the ball would follow the contour and kick slightly toward the hole. The shot paid off in spades. The ball landed on the green, darted toward the hole and rolled into the cup for an eagle that helped me to a 67 and a winning 272 total.

Another important factor in playing a recovery shot is to picture the shot and make your decision without too much hesitation. Indecision hurts because then you are playing your shot without the necessary confidence or concentration. Think ahead, get the picture in your mind and always try to save a shot, even if you are playing it safe for the next one. If a bogey is inevitable, accept it. When you play it safe for the easier shot that is to follow, you give yourself the chance to recoup. Avoid those near-impossible recovery shots that have to clear a large body of water or go under trees and over bunkers.

Last year at the Masters I put myself in trouble on my tee shot on the long second hole in trying to favor the left side of the fairway for a possible chance of getting on the green in two. Instead, I hooked deeply into the rough on the left and well into the woods. There went all thoughts of a birdie or eagle, and I had to figure how to start scrambling just to save a par. I had two alternatives. I could avoid the trees in front by playing backward toward the second fairway. But if I did this, I wouldn't be able to reach the green in three, so I explored the other. There was an opening through the trees to the adjacent eighth fairway that would advance me 150 yards *toward* the hole. I preferred this to going backward 50 yards. So after alerting both gallery and other golfers, I successfully punched the ball through the trees to the other fairway. This desperate maneuvering gave me a long but open shot to the green.

So, did I put that third shot on the green? No. It fell into a sand trap, and I thought "Here we go again." But knowing the sand shot quite well I did not fear it, and I knocked the ball out, close enough for a one-putt and a real zigzagging par. The score could have been much worse.

From the rough, or from a tight lie, proper club selection is important. Sometimes a green might be well within wedge distance, but a club with a cutting edge is needed. Using the wedge with its heavy flange might be defeating the purpose of what you are trying to do. Instead, use a club with a normal leading edge, one that will cut through rather than bounce off the ground and, at the same time, will produce a shot that will react the same way every time.

As valuable a club as the wedge is, one time it will hit the ball correctly and the ball will grab, the next it will run because the tall grass reduced the amount of backspin. Since you must be able to rely on either one or

For consistent results from heavy grass, select a nine-iron. Hit down sharply on the ball, keep knees flexed and head steady.

the other, use the nine-iron. You know it won't bite, but it will produce a shot with the same loft each time. It is easier to use and you can judge distance much more accurately.

Remember that indecision hurts. When you are in trouble, or even if you are not, take a club with enough loft to land you on the green and to stop or continue to run as the case dictates. The majority of the short approach shots call for your using nearly the same technique as you would from a perfect lie, in that the grip, stance and club are mostly the same. If you change the angle of the clubface to compensate for whatever trouble you might be in, be aware that it may affect your alignment, so make a corresponding change in your stance.

Once set, take the club back with the left arm and hand, without any body sway, hands in full control. The right elbow stays in close and the knees are flexed to permit a good hip and shoulder turn. At the top the

227

left shoulder is under the chin. As the downswing begins, the weight starts to shift back to the front leg with a lateral move of the hips. When the hands catch up to this action, the sensation is of the right hand hitting against a firm left side *although the left leads.*

Just before impact, the right hand "releases" as both hit into and through the ball. Contact is made sharply on the ball. Do not attempt to scoop the ball. The right arm becomes fully extended and follows the original line toward the direction of flight, the right side of the body is now completely relaxed and the hands finish high.

As you can see, scrambling takes art. It also requires "heart." I have seen golfers actually throw clubs in anger for having missed a shot. I don't know why. No one is immune to making errors, even the best of them. I know I've made my share, and I'm certain I haven't seen the last of such mistakes. But I hope you never resort to heaving the club. If you do, you are only berating an innocent party, your equipment, instead of the guilty one, you yourself. You are the one who put the ball wherever it winds up. Instead of blowing up, devote all your attention and talent to figuring out how you best can get out of the situation you alone put yourself in, without wasting any shots.

Any golfer who hopes to win or score well has to be able to come up with the recovery shot that will save him from those bad rounds. A man, no matter how good his game is, cannot hit that many greens and play so many good shots in a row and never be in trouble. But yet, as true as this is, it isn't always what happens.

At the tough Doral Country Club in Miami in 1964, Rex Baxter, in the final round, hit 18 straight greens in regulation, yet was able to make only one bird for a 71 total—higher than the last-day scores of winner Billy Casper's 70, runner-up Jack Nicklaus' 69 and Jay Hebert's 68, none of whom on that day was quite as consistent from tee to green.

The difference in most cases was those recovery shots up close enough, when the golfers got near the greens in two on the par-fives or when they missed on the others, to one-putt for their birdies and pars.

In summing up the art of scrambling, I'd like to reiterate these points:

1. Practice until you know exactly what can be expected of each club in your pitching arsenal.

2. Study the contour of the green and the grain to decide what type of shot is required, a chip and run, a lob pitch or a running pitch.

3. Pick out a spot on the green where you want the ball to land. Let

the forward momentum of the shot carry it to the hole.

4. Picture the shot exactly as it should come off.

5. Select the club that can do the job.

6. Concentrate completely on the job at hand.

7. Play the shot with complete confidence that you're going to make a success out of a bad situation.

And you will.

15. PRO POINTERS ON TROUBLE SHOTS

POPPING OUT OF TROUBLE

By Sam Snead

Several times in a round of golf, I find it necessary to play a cut shot to get best results out of certain situations. The circumstances may vary from shot to shot but the objective is always the same: to apply plenty of bite to permit as little roll as possible. *Cut shots are most effective when pitching out of heavy grass, playing off sandy surfaces (including traps) and shooting over obstacles to a tight pin position.* I would think that the average golfer would probably have five to six opportunities to use the cut shot during his 18-hole round. When playing the ball off sand, I address the shot with a fully opened stance and a slightly open clubface. The ball is opposite the left foot and the body is completely relaxed. *I take the club back outside the line of flight, applying an early wrist break. Supple wrists are necessary with this shot. The club is brought back somewhat more slowly than with a full iron shot. The downswing should also be from the outside in since this, in essence, is the cutting action.* When hitting a shot off grass, play the ball more toward the right foot with an open stance. The swing remains the same, but this time the ball must be hit first, the clubhead taking turf after contact.

NOT SO ROUGH

By Jim Ferrier

When in trouble, the average golfer too often relies on muscle rather than thought. This usually leads to the player taking a faster, harder swing than he needs. Most fast swings are flatter because there's a strong tendency to take the club back inside. In almost all instances, *when the ball lies in tall grass—for example, in grass two to four inches deep—the easiest way to get the ball airborne is by using a more upright swing.* The more upright action brings the club down into the ball at a sharper angle. I have found that by stepping three or four inches closer than normally to the ball I can effect trouble shots from rough. I find *I take the club away from the ball in a more straightaway fashion that puts me in good position to come down sharply into the ball and hit through it. This straightaway backswing, with the clubhead being elevated more quickly, gets the ball up fast.* To overcome any feeling of standing too close to the ball and possibly pushing it, transfer very little weight from the left to right leg during the backswing. (I have also found I can use a four-wood successfully from medium rough when I lay the clubface open slightly and use this more upright action.) The rough is not the exclusive property of the high-handicap golfer, and getting out is not exclusive with professionals. Just remember: Don't smash at the ball.

HITTING OUT OF CLOVER

By Retief Waltman

As most of you know, a golf ball hit from a clover lie has a tendency to run after it lands because the clover gets between the club and the ball, eliminating backspin. Flier lies, as the pros call a lie in clover or tufted grass, tend to make you hit the ball higher on the clubface than normally. This gets the ball up in the air more and makes it harder to control. *If a lie is so bad that you feel you can't help but hit a flier, take one club less to allow for the additional run.* Also, try to uncock the wrists sooner than usual, giving you almost the feeling that you are hitting from the top. This will enable you to avoid a cutting action and come into the ball at a shallower level.

PLAYING FROM THE ROUGH

By Ted Kroll

The first point to remember in executing an iron shot from the rough is to *keep the left hand more firmly on the club so it won't turn when it contacts the heavy grass.* The second thing to remember is to *make your backswing more upright.* It even helps to take the club back very slightly outside the line and play the shot as a slight cut shot. Avoid sweeping the club back. It helps you take a more upright backswing if you employ a slightly open stance. Reason for using a more upright swing than usual is that this helps a player get under the ball better. Now here's a third reminder: *use one less club than the shot would call for from a similar spot on the fairway.* A more lofted club will help a player get the ball in the air better and, coming out of the rough, the ball is likely to run more than usual. So a six-iron out of the rough will probably go as far as a five-iron from a similar spot on the fairway. And remember, be firm with your grip so the clubface won't close when the clubhead strikes the grass.

PLAYING THE HALF-SHOT

By Stan Leonard

The "half-shot" is roughly what the name implies—a stroke, usually with the middle or short irons, with which the ball travels perhaps 10 or 15 yards less than it would with the normal swing of the same club. It is a particularly valuable shot when playing into the wind. While it shouldn't be any more difficult than the full shot, there are several things to remember in its execution. *In the stance, the feet should be placed closer together. The club should be gripped an inch to an inch and a half down the shaft, bringing your whole body closer to the ball. Then the elements of the backswing must be restricted—its length, the wrist break and the weight shift. The wrist break should be no more than three-quarters of normal. What weight is shifted to the right side should never move fully onto the right foot, only to the inside portion of it. The best checkpoint here is to be sure the movement of the left heel off the ground is restricted.* Coming back to the ball, keep the downswing flowing and—this is very important—don't quit on the shot. Continue to a full follow-through. *Perhaps the most common error with players executing the "half-shot" is the tendency to get soft or sloppy with the hands in the grip and the wrist action. It's vital to maintain firmness throughout the swing.* You'll find on this shot that the ball won't sail as high because of the shorter distances being covered. But, because of the sharpness of the strike of the ball, you should get as much backspin and consequent "bite" as you do on a full shot with the same club. *The big thing to remember: Although the backswing is restricted on a half-shot, the follow-through must not be.*

GOLF EXTRA: DON'T PUSH THE PANIC BUTTON

By Peggy Kirk Bell

When that fine-looking shot takes a bad bounce and ends up in the rough, do not push the panic button! Instead, handle this situation with the same planning and judgment that might go into the preparation of dinner. The key words are planning and judgment.

By acknowledging the fact that everyone, regardless of handicap, has to contend with trouble shots of one form or another, you are preparing yourself mentally for a task that is largely psychological in the first place. And if you recognize your own ability and play within your skills, you will be able to diagnose the problem and score better because of it. This, of course, is the judgment phase.

The first order of business when we spray into the rough is the important one of evaluation. Check out the lie and the length and strength of the grass. If you think a club will have difficulty getting through because of the texture, eliminate from your mind all thoughts of distance. Select a lofted club and hit the ball onto the fairway in good position for the next shot. By the same token, if grass is relatively thin and the lie is good, you might find the five-wood the answer to your needs. This club has enough loft, head size and head weight to cut a path through the long grass and get the ball up quickly with the same swing used on the fairway. Again, however, it is a matter of judgment.

Ordinarily, I would not advise using any of the long irons or the woods from the rough unless the golfer is proficient with these clubs on the fairway. Too often I've seen players attempt to carry a ball 150 yards over water from the rough when their chances of doing so from a good lie would be no greater than 50-50. This is poor reasoning, of course. Unless circumstances dictate such a bold move, take the safe route. It isn't the most glamorous, but more than likely it will be the most successful. Get the ball back onto the fairway so that it will be in good position for the next shot. Do not compound trouble with more trouble, which is bound to follow the wild, unreasonable attempt.

240

Yet seldom does a golfing day go by but that someone regrets trying to pull off a miracle shot. Few realize that while the spectacular recovery may raise one's spirit for the moment, it also leads to rising scores—since

The lie in the rough must be very good before you can use a wood.

phenomenal shots of this type do not make for the sound foundation necessary for consistently good golf.

Be fair with yourself about the risk involved. Sometimes what's at stake dictates the action, although this isn't always true. It is now common knowledge that a promising young golfer might have tossed away his chance to win the 1962 U.S. Open by wasting four strokes trying to dislodge his ball from the branch of an evergreen at Oakmont, finishing the hole with a quadruple bogey 8. He lost a tie for the classic by two strokes. Once the shot has been diagnosed and the club selected, never let your confidence waver. Indecision at this point has actually ruined more recoveries than has the choice of clubs or any error in judgment.

Ordinarily, the ball that is hit from high grass will have overspin, and will roll much farther than fairway shots from the same distance. This has to be taken into consideration when choosing the club.

When the rough is high, take the club back in a sharper arc than usual. This will prevent the blade from getting snarled in the heavy grass.

I also recommend that the ball be played two inches back of the normal position, especially when loft is needed, or if hitting from a sandy lie. Hitting the ball a little more on the downswing will permit you to stay

241

Playing the ball two inches back of the normal position, take the club back in a more upright arc. A full shoulder turn is needed.

Hitting the ball more on the downswing permits you to stay with the shot longer, giving faster loft.

with the shot longer, eliminating the possibility of your giving it that lifting or scooping action which seldom works. And coming into quick con-

The trouble shot is not to be feared. Stay with it all the way, keep the grip firm and the head steady, and you'll be amazed at your consistent success.

tact with the ball will cause it to rise without catching more trouble.

Grip the club firmly but not too tightly, take the swing back slow and easy and, with irons, concentrate on hitting down and through the ball. The lie must be exceptionally good to consider using a wood at all. Any undue tension will result in a fast, jerky takeaway and a poorly executed shot. Keep the backswing short. I would compare it to a three-quarter punch shot swing. This will keep you from moving off the ball or swaying. Now, although the swing is a bit shorter, a full shoulder turn is quite necessary. Unless this turn is completed, the tendency will be to swing from the outside, resulting in a smothered shot.

The trouble shot is not to be feared. It does demand more concentration than shots from lush lies, but by "staying with the shot," keeping the grip firm and the head steady, you will succeed with amazing consistency.

VIII.   GOLF EQUIPMENT AND HOW TO CARE FOR IT

Undeniably, the golf equipment of today is the finest ever. A not surprising corollary to this statement is that it is also the most expensive. To protect your sizeable investment, it makes good sense to choose your equipment carefully and take care of it once you've purchased it. So that you may do this, the last section is devoted to the care, selection and history of golf equipment.

16.   GOLF GEAR NEEDS CARE

The golfer is a bigger enigma than the game itself, especially when the care of his equipment is concerned.

Who else would claim he loves the sport so much that his clubs are the first things he packs in the trunk of his car, underneath the weight of everything that goes on top? Then to straighten out the bent shafts, he takes matters into his own hands, a club breaks, and some manufacturer is faced with one of those touchy situations.

Who else would leave dirt and grime loaded with erosive chemicals on his clubs over the long winter months, then in the spring complain that they don't make 'em the way they used to? Or who else but a golfer would make a nuisance of himself by refusing—"because they don't feel right"—the first three sets his pro ordered especially for him, then blithely build up his grips, thus changing the long-sought original swing weight? The addition of one thirty-second of an inch to the grip reduces the swing weight by at least one point.

It is also a fact that an addition of one-eighth of an ounce to the club-head can change the swing weight one point, and a shaft that is one-quarter of an inch too short or too long can affect the swing weight two points up or down.

If this isn't enough, who else would bang his club into the ground in disgust over a bad drive, then spend hours on the practice tee trying to figure out why he is pushing or pulling his tee shots? An error of 1 degree at the outset can amount to as much as a 30-foot error at the target 200 yards away. This shattering experience to the club can also cause the inside wall of the shaft to flake off or to loosen some of the impregnated lead inside, making an audible noise as the club is taken from the bag and brought into address position. It has also been known to crack heads.

It is hard to ascertain what the average age of a set of golf clubs is in the United States. Guesses run anywhere up to 25 years. One educated estimate, however, has Americans buying new clubs every four years, and his

British cousin replacing his set every ten. This may or may not be absolutely accurate, but the investment in top-flight clubs is sizable, averaging about $104.00 for a set of woods, $173.25 for a set of nine-irons, $15.25 per wedge, plus about $15.00 for a putter. When you put it all together it spells "Brother!" So take good care of them.

Today's clubs differ greatly from those used as recently as ten years ago. Changes have taken place from end to end, although the nomenclature remains substantially the same. That is, a wood club still consists of head, insert, slug in sole, sole plate, screws, whipping, shaft with steps or gradations, grip and cap, while an iron consists of head or blade and hosel, shaft, either screwed in the hosel or held in place by a pin, shaft with steps or gradations, grip and cap. The woods are made of persimmon, laminated hardwoods or plastic, while the irons are either stainless steel or carbon steel.

Do not attempt to repair any damage to any of the components, and do not tinker with sole plate, shafts or heads. Major alterations are the job of skilled craftsmen qualified to handle the particular brand of club you are using. The repair of clubs has become so highly technical and demanding that at least one major manufacturer either trains its own men around the country or approves only those recommended by their district managers.

And above all, do not attempt to drill the heads of the sole plate screws when they are not easily removed with a conventional screw driver.

But when talk centers around just what is most unique in club manufacture, the vote has to go to the new woods which are pressure-impregnated to make them practically impervious to moisture, eliminating the chances of swelling, shrinking or warping as they were once wont to do. This is an important breakthrough: Not only does the head's stability remain intact; its swing weight is not altered by conditions. And they are much easier to keep clean. Where once the job of refinishing heads kept the lights on in the pro shops until the wee hours of the morning, nowadays such extra work is just about nonexistent.

To restore the gleaming, piano-top luster on the woods, apply a coat of furniture polish that also contains ingredients that will remove marks or stains, and follow with a good brushing with a soft cloth. If ball marks are or remain the problem, buff with the special rubbing compound of the type garagemen use to rub down the finish of the exterior of cars, giving them their high protective sheen.

247

But no set of woods will look good long if the golfer feels that head covers are too much of a bother. Due to the different lengths of the woods, if they are left uncovered, the top of the longer ones will rub against the sole plate of each of the shorter ones, cutting ugly and permanent scratches into the varnish painstakingly put there by the manufacturers. Head covers represent so little money compared to what they

are protecting: however, if they should get wet, remove them immediately, wipe off the woods, and replace the covers after they are thoroughly dry.

The neck whipping on the woods plays an important part in the club's strength, and some firms have changed from the thread to a plasticoated ferrule. But in either case pay close attention to keeping it in top condition.

You might appreciate the permanency, balance and maintenance ease of your present woods a bit more by this review of what had to be done to refinish a head just a few years ago. For one thing, the old finish had to be completely removed. This was usually done by soaking the club-head in a can of lacquer thinner, like acetone, and wiping off the finish as it peeled, continuing this operation until all the finish was cleaned off. Or if the job was real tough, the finish was scraped off with a hand scraper or piece of glass, sandpaper or steel wool. Imagine what this did to the club's swing weight and balance.

This also lessened the club's stability, because more often than not the filler, a paste that filled in the pores of the wood, was gouged out. Filler then had to be reapplied and allowed to set for some 15-20 minutes until the gloss disappeared, then wiped off with burlap, first across the grain, then lightly with the grain! The filler next had to dry for about 48 hours before the surface could be sanded. (If you are still so inclined to remove the finish from present-day clubs, do so with a leather wheel. The finish will disappear but the filler won't; in fact, the leather wheel actually burnishes the old finish back into the pores.)

The choice of finishes in those days was shellac, then lacquer, to the spar varnish and plastic finishes of today. Note these directions to be followed after the application of varnish: Lay on two full coats, not thick enough to sag or ripple. Sand lightly with garnet paper between coats. Allow the final coat to dry for three days.

Since dirt and mud will clean off more readily if the final coat is rubbed with pumice and linseed oil on a felt pad, it is advisable that you do so. Then rub with the grain but don't press hard enough to burn the top coat. When the gloss is gone, wipe clean with a dry cloth. An occasional wiping with a silicone cloth of furniture polish will keep the club new-looking all season.

The irons have also undergone some changes from as little as ten years ago, but the reasons for and the methods of keeping them clean remain the same. You cannot expect to play your best golf with clubs that are clogged with dirt or bits of grass; not only will the ball react crazily after being hit, but the actual "feel" of the club will be altered. To control the shot and get proper backspin on the ball, keep the scoring free of dirt and the clubface clean. Give the clubs a thorough washing in a soap and water solution, rinse and dry. That is all. Never use any harsh brushes, steel wool or abrasives, else you'll cut through the nickel-chrome plating, adding to the problem and ruining the club's appearance. This nickel-plating process is relatively new, having undergone extensive testing for ruggedness and corrosion resistance under the severest of conditions. It is comparable in thickness to that found on most automobile bumpers. Precisely 0.001-inch of nickel is electroplated over the carbon steel, followed by a chrome flash—the nickel to resist corrosion, the chrome flash for added appearance. All in all, one firm gives each iron a series of seven polishings, most of them to prepare the surface for the nickel coating, which lasts 30 minutes, and the chrome flash, which is given seven minutes. If the head is too rusted or pitted, arrange to have it returned to the manufacturer for repair or reheading.

Grip adjustment, breakage of clubs or bent shafts as pertaining to the woods apply to irons as well. Do not take any unnecessary chances: Have a qualified professional do the repairing, or have it sent back to the manufacturer.

Shoes. Your shoes also represent a sizable investment and require at least a minimum of attention. Remove grass and dirt from the spikes and soles before placing the clubs in your locker, carryall bag or car trunk. The temperature changes from outside to locker room and especially the variations in the trunk of the car would crack and stiffen any leather articles and tend to deteriorate rubber products. Keep the shoes treated and polished with a good leather conditioner, and always use good shoe trees to keep the shoes in shape. The spikes are a functional attachment. They're there to help you keep your balance and help execute the shot correctly. Check them periodically for loose or missing spikes. And wear shoes that fit!

Bag. Use a bag that is of ample size. Too often a small bag is used and the golfer has to jam his clubs into too small a space, raising havoc with the grips and endangering the shafts, as well. If the bag is of leather, treat it twice a year with a good leather conditioner to prevent cracking and excessive wear, and to add to its looks. Replace the strap when there is evidence of wear and avoid the inconvenience of a possible strap break in the middle of a round. Also check the condition of the zippers and avoid the expense of losing costly items. Do not allow anyone to sit on the bag and destroy the rings that give it its shape and strength, and be a little careful in inserting or removing clubs. To pull them out or thrust them in forcibly causes abrasions to the finish of both woods and irons.

Taking everything into consideration, the initial cost of top-grade golf equipment is rather high, but with little care the investment can be one that lasts a lifetime. You will play better, receive more for your money and enjoy the game to the fullest by getting the best and by keeping it in topflight condition.

17. WHAT YOU NEVER KNEW ABOUT THE GOLF BALL

No article of recreation is more abused, cursed and dispatched to such inglorious reward than the innocent-looking, dimple-faced golf ball. And no other ball or sports implement stirs up such all-out industrial warfare among the manufacturers who bid for a share of the $70,000,000 Americans spend for golf balls annually.

It is extremely doubtful, even in this Missile Age, if any designer or manufacturer will produce a ball that will fully satisfy the demands of all golfers of varying skills. Or one that will stay white and round and free of cuts and scuffs for as long as all golfers think it should. But, even with the odds stacked against them, the ball makers keep trying. As a result, the golfer winds up with a wide choice of balls that vary sharply in the theory of design and construction but conform to the strict limits on ball liveliness established by the U.S. Golf Association.

While it is understandable that Macy's does not tell Gimbel's, the secrecy surrounding the manufacture of golf balls is more like the security at a Minute Man missile plant. Each ball maker staunchly believes that his product is the best on the market, and he jealously guards the secrets of his theory and construction. Indeed, spokesmen for various brands generally seek anonymity and measure their words carefully when asked to explain their own philosophy of golf ball manufacturing.

"The design of a golf ball is a very complex matter," one maker states, "and in fairness to the golfer it should not be discussed publicly. The average golfer does not fully understand the technical details involved and he could easily become confused if he tried. The best way for a golfer to select the ball for his game is to go out and hit as many different brand balls as possible. The one that takes the longest walk to retrieve is the ball he should play with."

Many golfers do conduct their own tests in their search for the ball that is best for them, but probably just as many are attracted to a particular brand by an appealing feature. *High compression,* for instance, is a factor that is very attractive to many golfers, and numerous ball companies concentrate on this interest. It is also the source of much debate among ball makers as well as the basis for some confusion in the playing ranks. Indeed, in *Golf Magazine's* recent ball survey a large percentage of respondents indicated that they did not understand ball compression.

In order to fully appreciate any factor of the golf ball or of its performance, it would be wise to consider the basic structure of the ball.

The center of the ball probably has experienced more change than any other part of the modern ball. Over the years such varied substances as steel, fiberglass, pills, glass, rubber, silicone, water, blood, iodine, mercury, tapioca, dry ice, gelatin, arsenic and viscous pastes have been used in the center. Liquids generally have been encased in rubber covering.

After the center has been made, it is wound with rubber thread into a core. This winding is considered by some to be the greatest achievement in ball manufacture. The thread has been greatly improved through modern technology, and the chemicals that have been added make this new isoprene thread more uniform in feel and resiliency. The prestretched winding may be put on in one operation or in two separate but related stages. As it is applied, under tension, it stores up an abundance of energy. It's been said that there is enough energy in the thread to lift a 150-pound man two feet off the ground.

The center of the ball is placed under very high pressure by the winding. This effect can be illustrated by wrapping a rubber band around your finger. One turn and you can notice the pressure. If you build up several layers, it continues to get tighter and tighter. This is what happens to the golf ball center. The pressure on the center actually builds up to about 2,500 pounds per square inch. In other words, the center as a whole is sustaining a total pressure of from 7,000 to 8,000 pounds.

Since this is the heart of the operation, the manufacturers pay careful attention to the manner in which the windings are applied, the tension, the properties of the rubber and, of course, the retention of roundness. With each hit of the ball the thread will be stretched and some energy will be lost. Current tests indicate new highs in trueness, consistency and impetus ratings. Internal damage has been lessened, initial roundness is regained faster.

Such an emphasis on the winding could be misleading since the components relate one to the other. The finest innards would be of little value unless the cover belonged to the family. The cover stock is new and more resilient. It's more durable, without any loss of distance, and it also has more "feel." Once upon a time the cover, if thin, also was quite fragile. If the high-handicapper used golf balls of high compression and thin cover, he would nick the ball beyond use after three or four holes. Not so with today's cover.

The vast majority of golf balls are covered with balata gum—basically, a milky juice that is produced by the West Indian balata tree. When the substance dries it forms a hard, elastic gum not unlike the covering used for insulating wire and cable. While the balata cover marked a giant step forward when it was placed in general use about 25-30 years ago, ball makers have never stopped trying to come up with an even better cover. Right now a new covering, reported to be more resilient and more durable, is being tested in the laboratory. In the past year, one manufacturer departed radically from the standard process by developing a one-piece cover, which, it is claimed, is an improvement over the half-and-half covering.

The polyurethane paint which gives the ball its gleaming white finish is another sign of progress. One doesn't have to go too far back to recall how the golf balls hoarded over the winter months turned out to be tainted yellow when they were taken out of storage in spring. Or sometimes the leather of the golf bag inside the ball pocket discolored even new balls to a dull, used-looking shade. Now the golf balls are whiter to begin with, thanks to several coats of polyurethane paint and a final clear coat to lock in the whiteness. Today's balls show less wear and tear compared to those produced only a few years ago.

The dimples, while distinctive, are not intended to be a mere attractive design. They generally number 336 and they affect the aerodynamics of the flight of the ball. From the impact and force of the tee shot, backspin is imparted on the ball, causing it to rotate at a rate of 4,000 to 5,000 revolutions per minute. As the ball backspins, the rotation causes air to pile under the ball while sucking it away from the top of the ball. This creates a pressure underneath and a vacuum-like condition above —similar to the vacuum over the wings of an airplane in flight. This condition causes the rise of the ball and keeps it airborne. The number, size and depth of the dimples influence the lift and flight of the ball. If a change in the markings is made—even if the alteration is not more than one one-thousandth of an inch—a change in the flight of the ball would result.

Such an analysis might appear to the uninitiated to be a belaboring of the task of making a little white ball. But this hardly is the case. Indeed, some of the procedures have been minimized for clarity in the foregoing. One manufacturer claims that 85 separate steps are required in the production of his ball—a sobering thought for anyone who has teed up a new ball and neatly dispatched it to a watery grave.

The ball maker's burden, of course, is weighted considerably by the necessity of working within the restrictions imposed by the USGA. It would be quite simple to produce a ball that would travel 500 yards or more when properly hit. But Rules 2-3 of *The Rules of Golf* state that the velocity of a ball may not exceed 250 feet per second when tested on the USGA machine (allowing a reasonable tolerance of 2 percent). The desire to fulfill the average golfer's demand for a ball that will travel far and handsome, while staying within the USGA's limitations, has presented the manufacturers with a challenge.

In fairness to the governing fathers of the game, it should be made clear that some measure of flexibility is extended to the ball makers. There is no rule that specifies what materials must be used or in what amounts. The ball simply must be no smaller than 1.680 inches in diameter, and no heavier than 1.620 ounces (and, of course, pass the velocity test). Beyond these controls, the manufacturers are free to design any ball that will appeal to the golfer—and this is what they've been doing at a sizzling pace.

Ball compression has been somewhat of a magic word in ball-selling. Some ball makers use it in their sales presentations, while others protest that it is a grossly exaggerated and misunderstood factor.

Most ball men will point out, however, that compression—high, medium or low—is a factor in the makeup of all golf balls and that it plays an important role in helping the golfer achieve the maximum performance from the ball. Such a statement is true, but it is far too general in its scope. Indeed, it is almost impossible to deal with ball compression in broad terms and apply it to specific golfers.

In terms of the layman, compression relates to the hardness of the ball. In theory, the harder the ball, the less "give" it has and the more force is necessary to compress the ball and release the energy that is stored up within the ball. The distance the ball travels, therefore, is in proportion to the hardness of the ball and the velocity and efficiency of the mass (the clubhead) striking it. The split-second action at impact is the moment of truth—with the ball attempting to withstand resistance (the clubhead speed) and to snap back to original size and shape, and at the same time merging its own energy with the velocity of the club-head. Thus it might be said that when the ball of the golfer's choice (high, medium or low compression) reacts completely and correctly to the force of his swing (hard, medium or soft) the result should be maximum distance and maximum control.

It should be emphasized that the last statement is largely dependent on the efficiency of the swing or the consistent delivery of the clubhead to the ball on the proper plane, in the correct arc and at the proper speed. The fact that there is a wide variation in these factors among golfers makes it extremely difficult to fit a player to a ball of a specific compression through the use of any positive, slide-rule method. Even to observe the golfer's swing helps little. A golfer who appears to swing hard may be hitting with a lot of body, while a lazy-type hitter might have extremely fast hands. The tendency is to recommend a high-compression ball to the hard hitter. In this case, however, most ball experts probably would suggest that the lazy-type hitter with the fast hands use a ball that has a higher compression than the ball used by the body hitter to attain maximum ball performance.

It has been proposed more than once that a scientific device be used to measure accurately the swing of the golfer for the purpose of fitting him to the ball that would give him the highest degree of performance. Such a test would not be difficult to create. But in order to reach a useful conclusion, the golfer undergoing the test would have to consistently deliver the clubhead to the ball with a maximum of efficiency and power. Unfortunately, most golfers are not capable of such machine-like performance.

The USGA has called upon the men of science from time to time to gain more knowledge about the behavior of the ball, and also to improve and perfect the devices used for ball-testing. Some of the findings are not only fascinating, but they also throw an authoritative light on the claims and counterclaims of the ball industry. In 1957, for instance, the USGA engaged Arthur D. Little, Inc., scientific consultants in Cambridge, Massachusetts, to study the problems involved in creating a portable testing machine that would accurately measure ball velocity at the actual site of a championship tournament. Some of the key questions and observations of the study, in the USGA *Journal of Turf Management* in 1958, follow:

Can a certain type of ball give the long driver extra yards and yet not give proportionally extra distance to an average hitter?

Most golfers believe that a hard, tightly wound (i.e., high compression) ball does give the long hitter this advantage. This raises the question: What is the relationship between the compression of the ball and its performance when struck by the long driver and by the average driver?

Both these questions, says the Little study, seem to assume the length of the drive is more or less proportional to the velocity of the ball when it leaves the club. However, some theoretical scientists in Great Britain have callenged this assumption. Lord Brabazon of Tara voiced this view when he asked: "Does a long driver gain a disproportionate advantage because of a natural phenomenon having to do with a so-called critical Reynold's number?" (The Reynold's number is a physicists' term which describes properties of the relative motion of solid objects and fluids.)

You can think of this idea more simply as a disproportionately small air resistance encountered by a ball when it travels above a certain critical speed. If it's correct, the report states, then a driver whose ball can reach this magic velocity gets a bonus not available to his less powerful brother.

The researchers also inquired into what effect different types of clubs would have on the ball. Two of the questions raised are: "Does the long driver obtain a high velocity by using a heavier than normal club?" and "Does the improved shaft in the modern golf club bring about longer drives?"

While the report says it may seem obvious that a strong hitter strikes the ball more forcefully than the average golfer, it posed this: "Does the long driver by virtue only of superior skill obtain a more efficient impact with the ball or perhaps a better trajectory, thus getting a longer drive without a significantly harder stroke?" If so, it adds, then surely no one would want to reduce his relative advantage!

The USGA is constantly on the alert to the possibility that modern technology may soon make the present ball regulations obsolete. New synthetic materials might go into a ball that would make nonsense of the present velocity rule. With this in mind the report posed the question:

256

"Could wood, plastic and bone be replaced with a clubhead material that would give a more efficient impact with the ball?"

"In order to describe other phases of our attack on the golf-ball problem," the report states, "we must introduce here an important scientific concept. This is the so-called coefficient of restitution.

"This quantity with the imposing name we shall call 'e.' It is defined simply as the ratio of the relative velocity of the ball and the club after impact to their relative velocity before impact.

"Suppose, for example, that the club strikes the ball with a velocity of 200 feet per second. This number is a relative velocity before impact, because the ball is standing still (zero velocity). Suppose that the ball leaves the club after impact at a velocity of 250 feet per second, and that the club is slowed down to 120 feet per second. The relative velocity after impact is therefore 250—120, or 130 feet per second; this is the velocity with which the ball travels away from the club. Therefore 'e' has the value 130/200 or 0.65. (These are typical figures.)

"The ideal value of 'e' is 1; it can never be greater than this. It is sometimes thought (and this idea is common in elementary physics textbooks) that a perfect or ideal ball would have this ideal value of 'e.' According to our present thinking, however, this idea is erroneous; no golf ball could possibly be developed with $e = 1$.

"This, then, is one line of progress on the golf ball problem: We now know that the yardstick for measuring 'e' does not have a top reading of 1; it has something less. Actually a good golf ball—and it is hard to find a poor one nowadays—has an 'e' value of 0.75 to 0.80 for a very light impact (for example, when dropped on a concrete floor). For the hard-hit ball, the 'e' value drops to about 0.65. The big question is: How close are these values to the top of the yardstick? Here is one place where a theory is needed, only theory can tell us whether the present ball is close to ideal.

"Theory or no, there is no substitute for facts. Several of the questions can be answered only by actual measurements of the speed of the ball and the club, the carry of the drive and so on. Many of these measurements should be made in the laboratory, where wind and rain and muscles and nerves can be eliminated."

Also in this report, the Little organization revealed some conclusions it had reached after testing the driving of numerous golfers through the use of high-speed photographic measuring devices.

"An individual's clubhead velocity at the bottom of the stroke does not vary very much," the report states. "The ball velocity varies over a much wider range and seems to depend more on how squarely the ball is hit than on how fast the clubhead is traveling.

"To say that compression, within limits, has little effect on driving distance is not to say that compression makes no difference to the behavior of the ball. The photographs clearly show large differences; the softer ball is flattened more by impact with the club than is the harder ball. Even more apparent in the photographs is the fact that the ball stays in contact with the club for a longer time. . . . The golfer notices this effect in what he describes as the 'feel' of the ball; the high-compression ball gives a sharper reaction.

"The effect of compression is probably much more important for control than for distance. It seems likely that better control can be obtained with a soft ball than with a hard one. Because it flattens out more and covers a larger area of the club face at impact, the soft ball requires less critical accuracy at impact than the hard ball."

It should be pointed out that the golfers studied in this test were top tournament players, and it should be also noted that the Little organization suggested caution in interpreting the results of the study. It also should be noted that most of the balls sold are of average compression (soft to medium). Those with a high compression (hard) usually are marked by the manufacturer either by compression number or with a specific symbol or color.

The USGA spends a goodly sum of money each year just to test each golf ball on the market to see that they meet with the specifications for tournament play. The balls are tested at the United States Testing Center in Hoboken, New Jersey, for size, weight and velocity. First the balls are tried on for size and rejected if they are smaller than the required 1.680 inches in diameter. Next they are weighed and must not exceed 1.620 ounces. Finally, they're tested for velocity to determine initial speed—the time required for the ball to go a certain distance off the tee.

The sport is determined there shall be no rabbit ball scandal such as hit baseball in 1961. Francis Ouimet, Walter Hagen, Bobby Jones and Babe Ruth (on the golf course) hit the same ball as Arnold Palmer, Gary Player, Jack Nicklaus and Roger Maris (on the golf course).

In fact, golfers have been hitting the same type pellet since 1901, but don't call that decadence. The idea is to keep the game constant so records can't be questioned. They cited smaller parks, poorer pitchers and a souped-up ball among other things when Maris hit his 61 home runs. They can say what they want about baseball, but golf refuses to allow its critics to attribute improved play on the ball. Actually, it would be easy to squeeze a rabbit into a golf ball—soup it up to gain added distance without changing the size or weight by winding the inner rubber more tightly. That's why the velocity test.

All this doesn't mean that the game hasn't been all balled up with controversy. In England, they swat a ball that is 1.62 ounces and 1.62 inches in diameter and there are reformists—the venerable Gene Sarazen, for one—who say the ball should be made uniform since British and United States golfers have their Common Market.

Manufacturers' spokesmen have said that the new thread has been the big improvement in the ball. Some say it's the polyurethane paint, others the more durable cover, or the methods of winding, but little mention is made of the center. Yet on the market today there are centers of great variety. Apparently the manufacturers select a center that relates with the other components to produce the "feel," the "click" and the "performance," feeling that the center itself will not produce additional distance. Indeed, it seems to have become a part of the over-all picture—a component selected and designed to insure trueness of roll and perfect roundness. Thus it does deserve to be the heart of the golf ball. While once it was a factor in allowing the energy of the hit to continue through the interior, today it appears that few golfers can generate the velocity that will penetrate through the newly activated cover and deep into the tightly wound, highly energized thread, let alone reach the middle of the ball.

The secrecy of ball manufacture is such that in many plants even the men who are working on the ball do not know what goes into its makeup. On the days the thread is wound, the area where the machines are located is off limits to all but a few trusted workers. The time cycle of the operations is heavily guarded, and never are the ingredients that go into the makeup of the thread, cover stock or even the paint revealed.

There is reason for this. The making of a golf ball is a highly technical operation, and any alteration in the work flow, or difference in procedure, or change in formula of the cover stock, paint application or curing time could indicate the new direction any manufacturer might be headed.

259

With so many persons involved in so many steps in the making of a ball, such secrecy ofttimes appears to be ludicrous, but never is it unnecessary. The word that a new ball is on the market that will do everything the golfer desires can spread like wildfire. And there is nothing swifter-moving than a golfer who wants that certain something that will cut strokes from his game! The manufacturers are meticulous about their products. Recently one major manufacturer, prideful of his reputation and mindful of his market, deliberately burned some 60,000 dozen quality golf balls because they didn't meet his specifications.

The golf balls used in the era before 1848 consisted of a leather cover stuffed with a hatful of feathers. Three pieces of bull's hide were stitched together. Boiled feathers were stuffed into the ball. When the feathers dried they expanded against the cover. A rubbing process produced a white cover. This complicated process of ball production was reflected in the price. Based on the current value of our dollar, the "featheries" would have cost about $5 each. But, everything considered, they were extremely lively. Indeed, a Frenchman, Samuel Messieux, reportedly drove one 361 yards in 1836.

The "featheries" lasted until 1848, when some enterprising Scotsman introduced the "gutty," a smooth, solid ball molded from gutta-percha, a tough thermoplastic gum extracted from the bark and leaves of palaquium trees native to Java. This ball was a real improvement over the feather ball because it was more stable in the wind and less affected by dampness.

The present-day golf ball had its origin in 1899 when Coburn Haskell of Cleveland invented and patented the rubber wound ball. The live rubber center, the winding of rubber bands, and a cover of gutta-percha, later changed to balata, comprise the three components that persist to the present day.

The "bounding billies," as the new balls were called, were too lively around the green, and the distance gained was not enough to offset this disadvantage. But improvement in playability was rapid, accompanied by a change in golf club design and a new and more efficient golf swing. The rubber balls quickly put the old gutties out of existence, and in less than a year the guttie became nothing more than a relic.

New centers, tighter winding and thin covers made the golf balls go farther, and in 1922 the USGA set its foot down on any more revolutions and innovations. The ball was standardized and made lighter and larger, an action necessary to save the golf courses. Many recalled the distress of the early 1900's with the Haskell ball, when courses had to be lengthened. It meant millions of dollars to the clubs compelled to purchase new land for the extended courses.

Thus the USGA has established a distinct limit which serves the dual purpose of maintaining golf's competitive standard while challenging the ingenuity of golf ball manufacturers. A heavier ball will go farther, but it would be illegal. A smaller ball likewise would go farther and likewise would be illegal. This means that the makers have to concentrate elsewhere to produce a ball that gives the good "click" when hit solidly, that stays whiter hole after hole, and one that lasts round after round while staying round. This is actually being done. Look again at the ball you've been using. Even though it might be the "wrong" one for your game, the overwhelming odds are that it has remained cut-free, whiter and rounder longer than its counterpart of as recently as five years ago. For this we can credit the pride of the manufacturers, the quality demands of the golfing public, the competition among the professionals and the policing of the United States Golf Association.

18. THE GOLF GRIP REVOLUTION

It's not surprising the average golfer gives so little thought to his grips. He has enough to do remembering *how* to grip to be concerned with *what* he's gripping.

And it's not just the high-handicapper who tends to fall into this trap, as the following shows.

There was once a golfer who played to a six-handicap on a very tough course. Bill, as we'll call him, played with grips he had worn down to the steel under his right thumb and forefinger and under the middle and ring fingers of the left hand.

In preparing for a major club tournament, his professional persuaded him to have new ones put on.

The result was an unheard-of disaster. Bill played so badly in the match he was beaten five and four. The new grips worked well enough in practice, he said, but when it came to playing under pressure in the tournament, he lost all feel in his clubs.

While it may or may not have been a good thing for Bill to play with such worn grips, the grooves he'd made did at least give *him* a solid feel. Grips are a very personal thing. Another point, which we'll get to later, is that the serious golfer should not assume that the conventional round and tapered grip is *necessarily* the best for him. But worst of all, Bill just didn't stop to think what a change of grip could mean to his game.

Take a leaf from the grip designer's book. With every major change in the equipment or technique of the game, he has had to think out a new grip to conform.

Back in the days of the gutty ball and hickory shaft grips were much larger than the ones on your present clubs. Club craftsmen covered the wooden shaft with several layers of woolen cloth before winding on the outer layer of sheepskin. The reason for all this padding was that, though the gutty went off sweetly enough if struck squarely, you got quite a shock if you mis-hit it.

This state of things prevailed from the 1850's—when the gutty ball won out over the original "feathery"—until around the turn of the twentieth century, when both a new method of holding the club and a new ball demanded a thinner golf club grip.

Before Harry Vardon's prowess popularized the overlapping grip, golfers used a double-handed grip with both thumbs more around rather than on top of the grip. This was the most natural way to hold the thick grip of the day.

But when golfers began to overlap on the thick grip and put the upper thumb more on top of the shaft, the result was rather uncomfortable and a thinner grip was called for.

What made the thinner grip possible was Dr. Haskell's rubber-core ball. Unlike the gutty, it gave you little or no shock however badly you hit it.

The grip resulting from these two developments was much thinner and consisted of cotton fabric wrapped around the hickory shaft, then covered with leather.

A change in golf technique caused still further reduction in grip thickness. The St. Andrews swing was abandoned and the upright swing came into vogue. The club now entered the hands at a greater angle than in the outmoded flatter swing and the club was held more in the fingers. This is the same swing, in essence, that has continued up into modern times.

The introduction of the steel shaft posed another problem for grip designers. As with the gutty ball, the steel shaft gave you quite a sting if you hit the ball inaccurately. Indeed, if it had not been for the rubber-core ball which absorbed quite a lot of the shock, steel shafts might never have become popular.

However, steel shafts were stronger and lighter than the old hickory shafts and were less inclined to twist during the downswing. These qualities were too good to pass up, and grip designers had to come up with a more shock-absorbent grip.

Over the years grip designers have tried various listings (or undercoverings) under leather grips. One of the earliest was covering the steel shaft with friction tape, felt, cotton fabric and then paper to get the right shape. Another was using paper alone. However, paper by itself made for a hard, unyielding grip.

Perhaps the simplest—and cheapest—listing has proved to be rubber-cork composition. It can be molded to shape, slipped on in one operation and the leather then wound on top. It gives a resilient feel to the grip and acts as a shock absorber to the force of the hit. This method is also much cheaper than applying cotton listing, which calls for highly skilled labor in the winding.

Nor have the leather tanners been idle in improving the playing characteristics of leather. At one time leather exposed to temperatures of 50 degrees or less used to harden. Today grips have been tested down to freezing point without losing their tackiness and will not lose feel in very hot weather.

Up till a few years ago, grips used to lose their tackiness after two or three years and needed a dose of castor oil. Now, special antioxydizing material is put in the grips and their tackiness will last for the life of the club. Dirt can still impair tackiness, but you can remedy this by washing the grips in mild soap and water.

Previously, rain was quite a problem for leather grips. They absorbed water (or perspiration), which added to the weight of the grip. This upset the club's swing weight by making the head feel lighter than normal. That's now a thing of the past as the modern leather grip is treated with special resins so that it does not retain moisture. Incidentally, the best way to retain your grip on leather in very heavy rain is to use a light cotton glove.

Another solution to the problem of gripping steel-shafted clubs is the rubber-cork composition grip. The first synthetic grips appeared just before World War II and have been with us ever since. Today they share half of the market with leather grips.

At first these grips also had their problems. Rubber alone was used and this had several disadvantages. It was too hard on the hands and caused blisters. It was also heavy and tended to make the head feel too light.

However, in 1948 a new grip made of a rubber and *cork* compound came on the market. It was much lighter than the rubber-only grip and also cured the blister problem. The cap and grip were made in one piece—a major advance—and required only three operations to make. In comparison, a regular leather grip needed about 16 operations.

Through the years, manufacturers have come up with many shapes of grip other than those with circular cross-sections.

One reason for this was that the club twists during the swing and this could turn the club in the hands. The other was that many golfers found it difficult, while swinging, to feel their hands were in the correct position. It's a fact that if you were to blindfold even an expert golfer and then hand him a club with a round grip, he couldn't square the club with the line of flight without first placing it on the ground.

Today there are numerous specially shaped grips on the market to take care of this. Some have flattened sides, others have a flattening at the top of the grip, still others have a rib on the bottom or top and bottom of the grip. On putters you can now get an almost bewildering variety of shapes. There are even grips with forms which place the hands or fingers in more or less locked-in positions, but these are strictly training grips. USGA rules prevent their use in competition.

The golfer also needs grips with good traction, grips that will not slip or turn in any weather. Moisture, whether from perspiration or the elements, must also be dispersed.

On the cork and rubber grips, the golfer gets traction from the material itself and the surface design. Pockets or indentations in the grip displace moisture and prevent slipping, without the golfer having to grip harder.

Leather grips rely on their tackiness to get traction, with an assist from the small round perforations made in the leather. These tiny holes help drain away sweat, etc., which then evaporates in the atmosphere. The edges of the grips are skived (thinned) so that when they are wound on they form ridges or grooves down the grip which also help to stop slipping.

Perhaps you've wondered why the grip tapers down from top to bottom. This has been the conventional shape for grips from time immemorial. The reason can be better understood by making this experiment.

Stretch out your arms, with the hands together, as when holding a club. Your arms form a "V" and you'll note the opening in your hands —where the grip would be—is conically shaped and naturally fitting the conventional grip. This conical grip, therefore, is designed to conform to the hands in action.

Recently, however, this concept has been challenged by at least two new grips, both, funnily enough, designed by amateur golfers.

One grip tapers at both ends. Thus the left hand grips the thinnest part of the grip and right hand, the thickest. This, the inventor claims, strengthens the grip of the left hand—many weekend golfers let go with the left—and cuts out the right hand enough to stop it overpowering the left.

The other grip tapers down from the top of the grip in the usual way, then bulges out under the right hand in an hourglass shape. By giving you twice the amount of grip under the right hand, its creator says, you only have to hold it half as tight with the right to get the same firmness of grip you got on the conventional grip.

Both of these new grips come in rubber composition at the present. However, there is no good reason why they can't be made in leather. A rubber listing of the desired shape could be devised and the leather wound on top in the usual way. This would be, it is true, two operations instead of simply slipping on a rubber grip in one. However, available to the professional right now is a slip-on leather grip (on a rubber foundation) of the conventional taper. So if these novel grips catch on, it's likely you'll be able to get them both in rubber and leather.

A word about grip sizes. Most grips come in standard sizes, large, medium and small. These will vary about a tenth of an inch with the size of the shaft. While tournament professionals can feel a difference of only a few thousandths of an inch in diameter, most golfers will find new clubs equipped with grips which fit their hands. A rough guide: If the tips of the fingers on the left hand bite into the palm, the grip is too small; if a sizable amount of grip appears between the palm and the fingertips, then the grip is too large. Those with special problems should have grips installed by their local pros.

In choosing new clubs, or new grips for your clubs, remember this: Your grips should feel good in your hands—at all times, in all climates. They should have a good, positive feel and not hurt your hands. They should enable you to grasp the club correctly, firmly and easily to maintain control, power and clubface alignment.

So think, think, think about your grips. So that next time you swing, you can *safely* forget about them.

GOLF EXTRA: THE CHAMP'S CLINIC

PROBLEM: Suddenly, I am not able to keep a firm grip on the club at the top of my swing. It loosens in the palm of my left hand, in the thumb and forefinger of my left and little finger of my right hand. Shortening my backswing only disrupts my rhythm.—Dave Bassett, Napoleon, Ohio.

ANSWER: The pressure in the left hand should be felt in the last three fingers. Shortening your backswing has to help. It would seem as though you are not getting your shoulders to turn enough. Worry less about the length of the swing going back, grip firmly but not too tightly in both hands, improve your footwork and concentrate more on a better body turn. Your timing will develop and your accuracy will begin to improve.

PROBLEM: My tee shots seem to float rather than bore through the air and land with little or no roll. This means I have to hit long second shots to the green. What could this be?—Mark Musolf, FPO, San Francisco, Calif.

ANSWER: You might be at fault anywhere from stem to stance, fore and aft, and it would do you little good to pick out any one of the possible errors. Instead, I'll mention that the ball you are using may be the guilty party. Sometimes a golfer will use a ball that has too low a compression rating. If it is too soft, it will flatten out at impact and won't recover its original shape soon enough. It could travel in this state for some distance, usually low at the outset, then climb until, when it does return to original size, it'll complete its high arc and fall with little forward roll.

PROBLEM: I've been told that most of the top players play all their shots off their left foot. Is this true? If so, is this good?—Butch Loeloff, Columbus, Ind.

267

ANSWER: Mostly true because it is good. The ball that is played up forward takes advantage of the full arc and the greatest clubhead speed, with a higher degree of accuracy resulting. A movement that often goes unnoticed, even by the better players, is the gradual creeping up by the golfer until he is playing the ball back nearly opposite his right heel. He finds it almost impossible to get the club into *and* through the ball and, despite any body or hand action, he loses distance and control.

PROBLEM: *How can you get backspin on a trap shot to make it stop more quickly on the green?—D. Wackenhuth, North Caldwell, N. J.*

ANSWER: Assuming that you are following through after hitting into that spot about two inches behind the ball, take the sand wedge straight back from the ball (or slightly outside), played off the front foot, in a three-quarter swing, with both your stance and the clubface open. With all things considered, such as texture of sand, type of green, firmness of swing, etc., you should get all the action you want. To move the spot any closer to the ball would be too dangerous.

PROBLEM: *The phase of the golf swing that confuses me most is the backswing. Should you drag the clubhead back low to the ground without supinating or pronating, or should you cock the wrists at the beginning? Which would promote the most powerful and consistent golf swing?—Carl Surtman, Toledo, Ohio.*

ANSWER: For day in and day out reliability, the swing with the least movable parts will be the better one for you. This means taking the club back low, but without any body sway, with no wrist break the first 10 to 12 inches, and no break in the arc of the clubhead. Keep the swing as simple as you can.

PROBLEM: *By following the suggestion of a local pro and keeping my clubface square, I hit the ball straight but not far. By being "open" and then hitting with my right hand at impact, I get much more distance but sometimes slice or push the ball to the right. I am 5'8" and not too strong, but naturally I like to get as much distance as possible. How?—John Lyons, Detroit, Mich.*

ANSWER: Distance without accuracy seldom wins. The "wild man's" successful rounds are as inconsistent as his tee shots. You have described the difference between the modern "one piece" method of keeping the clubface square throughout and the old way of pronating, or rolling the wrists on the backswing which required similar action going into the ball. The American professional prefers the former because less can go wrong. I would suggest you, too, adopt the method your pro suggested, stay with it until it is thoroughly tested, and your timing and rhythm will take care of additional distance.

PROBLEM: *When I am in the groove hitting my six-, seven- and eight-irons, the feeling is that I'm hitting the ball with the left shoulder. Is this a good feeling? I play from a five handicap.—Fred Altergoot, Kenosha, Wisc.*

ANSWER: Your handicap has convinced me that hitting the ball with the left shoulder is a good feeling. Apparently, you have coordinated the movement of your hands with good footwork, the right elbow brushes the right hip properly, keeping the right shoulder inside the line and the clubface square to the ball. Retain this coordination and you'll stay on target.

PROBLEM: *What is the best way to keep a golf glove tacky? Mine always cracks.—David Meyer, Saginaw, Mich.*

ANSWER: Use any of the quality leather preservatives now available to soften the glove, prevent its cracking and restore essential oils. Some will even waterproof it.

PROBLEM: *When I keep my left foot down like I'm told in stories by professionals, I only get about 150 to 175 yards. But when I rear back and let the left foot go, I get 200 to 215 yards. Should I let the left foot go anyway? I'm a 16 handicap.—R. C. Blakeman, Seattle, Wash.*

ANSWER: If this action is really the secret of getting an extra 50 yards on tee shots, can you imagine what the golfers of the world would look like? It would almost be enough to restore the Polo Grounds. What many pros suggest is to keep the left heel on the ground as you go into the takeaway, or, at the most, lift it only about an inch, enough to see some daylight. Feel some pressure on the inside and toe of the left foot, and your left knee should be pointing toward the back of the ball. Maintain solid footwork on both the backswing and the downswing, develop timing so the clubhead is accelerating at its fastest speed just before impact, and you will get all the distance you will ever need.

PROBLEM: *Hitting behind the ball is called "hitting it fat." This I know, but what causes it and what is the cure?—Charles Fiorillo, Buffalo, N. Y.*

ANSWER: We prefer the positive approach to the negative, but some of the causes are: dropping the right shoulder, faulty weight shift, quitting on the shot, bad footwork, including stiff knees, or keeping the weight on the right side. Assuming that there is nothing wrong with your eyesight, try to sense the whereabouts of the clubhead at all times, make certain it goes away from and returns to the ball in a smooth, unbroken arc. Your hand and body action should be such as to encourage this evenness of motion. Do not try to sweep the ball but, instead, hit down on it. Stay with the shot all the way. A steady head position, a firm left side and a good weight shift will insure a solid hit.

PROBLEM: *All my irons go straight but a mile high and I can't figure out why. I actually hit the two-iron higher than a lot of golfers hit a seven. I am 5'7" tall, have a very upright swing. Any suggestions?— Henry Burton, Sherman, Texas.*

ANSWER: Unless your arms are extremely short, your height would make an upright swing difficult, unless all of your weight is on the right side, or you are swinging from your toes, or only with the arms far out from your body. Try flattening the plane a little. Bring the hands in closer to the body, shift weight smoothly, pivot more and grip firmly. Hit down and through the ball without any unnecessary effort and follow through.

PROBLEM: *I am 17, shoot around 74, but my distance is poor. I feel it is because I don't use much hip turn. I've been told my upright swing is good, but I'd like to know how to delay my hip action.—Dud Holland, Ruston, La.*

ANSWER: You don't want to *delay* the hip. Get it to work for you. Move it out laterally toward your target as far as you can on the downswing; in fact, stretch the entire left side with your left shoulder raised a bit and hit the ball with good hand action. With rhythm and balance you'll be hard to hold back.

PROBLEM: *Is it not logical for a player of medium or short height to choke up on the grip to be more effective out of sand traps? Burying the*

270

feet firmly in the sand brings my hands closer to the sand and further reduces my already short height.—John M. Larson, Springfield, Mass.

ANSWER: Yes, *anytime* your feet are lower than the ball, make a proportionate change in your grip. However, do not shorten the grip just for the sake of doing so, especially if your sand trap lie is similar to one from the fairway. Remember, unlike the fairway shot, you *want* to hit the ground (sand) first.

PROBLEM: I am confused about how club length is ascertained. Using the driver, is it determined from the end of the shaft to the bottom of the club, to the top of the club, or just the visible part of the shaft? And how does one measure the distance you are standing from the ball. From the left toe? How far do you stand from the ball?—C. E. Deeds, Houston, Texas.

ANSWER: Club length is measured from the base of the heel to the tip of the shaft. The distance one stands from the ball is normally measured from an imaginary line drawn between the tips of the toes, parallel to the line of flight, and the ball. I personally stand both close enough and just far away enough to make solid contact with the ball consistently.

PROBLEM: Instead of having a grooved putting stroke, I have a looped one in which all putts are pulled to the left. How can I overcome this? —Ronnie Farhood, Wheaton, Md.

ANSWER: The fault could lie with your stance, the length, loft or lie of your putter, the position of your head and hands, or with body movement. On the practice green try keeping your eyes directly over the ball, take the putter back low to the ground, keep the blade square to the line, and, moving only the hands, wrists and arms, learn how to stroke the ball the same way every time. Don't look up until you hear the ball fall into the hole. It'll be worth the effort.

PROBLEM: I am a relative newcomer to golf, but I hit my driver straight and in the air. My trouble is getting loft with the three-wood. I even turn up the clubface.—Randy Anderson, Placentia, Calif.

ANSWER: Your solution is causing the problem. Let the sole of the club rest flat on the ground, with the bottom line at right angles with your line of flight, and assume your stance (you may use a waggle or a forward press), then swing into the ball. The design of the club will do the needed lifting.

PROBLEM: I have read golf ball advertisements describing compression ratings of 80 plus, 90 plus and 95 plus. Would you explain this business of compression to me?—Gary Jones, San Francisco, Calif.

ANSWER: Compression ratings pertain to the tension of the winding. Usually, the tighter the ball is wound, the higher the compression. I say "usually" because much of this is dependent upon the materials and methods used. This may vary with different manufacturers, but each is obliged to produce a ball not more than 1.620 ounces in weight, not less than 1.680 inches in diameter, a velocity not greater than 250 feet per second, with a 2 percent tolerance when tested in 75 degree temperature on the USGA's apparatus. The higher the compression, the more force is required to release the energy and the farther the ball *could* travel. Unless the golf swing is powerful and well grooved, however, this energy will not be released and would, in a sense, work against you. In this case, a ball with a lower compression would spring back into action easier, giving more distance.

PROBLEM: I have trouble keeping my eye on the ball when I drive and consequently top them. How can I learn to hold my head still and hit the ball square?—Art Castellazzo, Orange, Conn.

ANSWER: The head has to remain the axis of the swing and it should stay behind the hit. Some slight movement is almost necessary to keep you from becoming too tense, thus restricting proper turning, but under no circumstance let the head get in front on the downswing. You might find it helpful to maintain your balance by concentrating on pivoting around a "point" centered in the base of your neck.

PROBLEM: How can I keep from getting too much loft on my irons? I always sky them and fall short of target.—Allen Sproxton, Manitoba, Canada.

ANSWER: Your hands are not coming into the shot soon enough, your weight is probably on the right side and on the heels too much, and, if you're playing winter rules, you just might be giving yourself too good a preferred lie.

272

PROBLEM: *I was taught that the more loft to the club, the more open your stance is. Lately I've had the tendency to pull these irons. How should I compensate for this?—Tom Plakias, New York, N. Y.*

ANSWER: The more loft to the club, the shorter the club, the closer you play the ball and the narrower your stance should be. Get your feet closer together and play the shot directly at the pin. Be sure that the left side doesn't swing out or around too much before the hit.

PROBLEM: *Any explanation of the punch shot and the lob with the wedge will be appreciated.—R. L. Hester, Cuthbert, Ga.*

ANSWER: The wedge is a versatile, extremely valuable club. Knowing how to use it for both the punch and the lob will cut many strokes from your score, but you must give yourself time to practice with it. Try to punch a low wedge by playing the ball back off the right heel from a slightly open stance, using no more than a three-quarter swing, with little wrist break. Keep the hands ahead of the clubface and you might square off the blade, too. To lob the ball, play it forward, open the stance and the blade a bit and, with a good shoulder turn, hit down into the ball crisply. Follow through completely.

PROBLEM: *How do you hit the downhill trap shot?—Frank Zodda, Tenafly, N. J.*

ANSWER: Much depends on the steepness of the decline, just as does the downhill lie from the fairway. Open your stance and play the ball back toward the right heel because you'll be hitting your target before the lowest point of the arc is reached. Take the clubhead back and up rather abruptly and, with an open face, hit the sand about two inches behind the ball and follow through normally. As your swing continues, the clubhead will stay close to the sloping sand. The steeper the downhill lie, the more difficult the shot. Keep your eyes focused on your target behind the ball and get the clubhead into that spot. Do not be forced by the downhill pull into lunging and, above all, have faith.

PROBLEM: *Using the driver, I'll slice the ball 50 yards. The same with the brassie, but with the Numbers 3 and 4 woods, I'll hit high, 200-yard shots straight down the middle. The more I practice, the more I want to throw away the driver. What's the solution?—Murray O'Neal, Riverside, Calif.*

ANSWER: Are you swinging from the right side, with the weight on the heels? The correction does not seem to be in the loft of the clubs you are having trouble with. Most drivers have a face angle of 10 to 11½ degrees, and the brassie or 2½ wood from 13 to 14½ degrees. If the swing weights are the same, it is something you yourself are doing or not doing that is causing the poorly hit tee shots. Do not overpower this shot. Slow down your backswing, improve your balance, pivot and swing through the ball.

PROBLEM: *I am losing power by uncocking my wrists too soon. How can I delay this action?—Charles Lipson, Marks, Miss.*

ANSWER: Relax the tension and improve your timing and footwork. You are swinging from the top. Do not begin to snap your wrists into the ball until your hands have reached hip level or lower on the down swing.

PROBLEM: *If a golf ball touches any part of a line that is used to mark out-of-bounds, is the ball considered to be out?—Walter Machowski, New Bedford, Mass.*

ANSWER: The Rules of Golf, Section II, Definitions, state: "When out of bounds is fixed by a line on the ground, the line itself is out of bounds. A ball is out of bounds when *all* of it lies out of bounds."

PROBLEM: *I've read that while playing from a sand trap you should not use a pitching wedge but a sand wedge. If you do not have a sand wedge, what do you advise to use from the trap?—Art Ross, Edmore, Mich.*

ANSWER: The utmost skill. Seriously, the sand wedge has the largest flange, making it most suited for trap shots. The flange, which makes contact with the sand before the leading edge does, prevents the leading edge from digging too deeply and stopping the swing. There is also a bit of a flange on the pitching wedge. If you own neither, well, maybe you'll have to use the utmost skill.